THE HISTORY OF MUSIC MACHINES

THE HISTORY OF MUSIC MACHINES

Drake Publishers Inc

New York · London

Published in 1975 by
Drake Publishers, Inc.
381 Park Avenue South
New York, N.Y. 10016

ISBN: 0-87749-755-9
LC: 74-22565

Printed in the United States of America

1234567890

CONTENTS

Introductory notes by Erik Barnouw and Irving Kolodin   **9**

Music Machines—American Style   **17**

Music and Machines in the 19th Century   **19**

Music Parlors—Public and Private   **31**

Music Machines in the Home   **53**

Acoustic and Electric Recordings   **71**

The Impact of Radio   **85**

Movies and Music   **99**

The Jukebox Craze   **107**

Semper Fidelity   **115**

Electronic Instruments and Music   **127**

Bibliography   **138**

FOREWORD

In the last century in the United States music has been democratized. The invention, manufacture, and diffusion of music machines have spread the opportunity to hear all sorts of music to nearly everybody. The sounds of music have become a much less special experience. Almost any sort of music can be heard at almost anyplace and almost any time. This is an achievement, not only of technology, but of merchandizing and advertising.

In this exhibit the visitor can see how the machinery of music-making has developed, can have a few clues to how international the story has been, and can glimpse some of the eye-appeal that helped arouse the desire of Americans to Own Their Own. An exhibit such as this can loosen our imaginations to new possibilities of sound which are as hard for us to conceive as today's Hi-Fi would have been to our grandfathers. It should remind us that progress means a willingness to embrace the unfamiliar, a quality which Americans have seldom lacked.

While the main stages in the development of music machines can be sampled here, barely a clue can be given to the changing styles and fashions in the composing and performing of music. Have music machines sharpened our awareness of the actual sounds of music, or have we come to take these for granted, like air-conditioning? It is perhaps too soon to say whether the enticing opportunity to reach almost anybody almost any time has stirred into being great composers to match the machines. In this exhibit we see the remarkable technology that has made possible new experience for the layman and a vast new reach for the composer.

Daniel J. Boorstin
Director
The National Museum of History
and Technology

ERIK BARNOUW ON BROADCASTING

While noting the rise of radio and television as music machines, we should perhaps do a moment of obeisance to their ancestor, the telephone. Though not usually thought of as a "music machine," it foreshadowed in its first days much of broadcasting history. Alexander Graham Bell, in his telephone demonstrations of 1876-77, constantly included musical performances as well as speech. Thus an audience in Boston was enabled to hear, via telephone, selections from *The Marriage of Figaro* performed in Providence; and an audience in Providence heard "The Star-Spangled Banner" from Boston. The telephone was expected to provide such entertainments to the home on a regular basis. An 1877 popular song, "The Wondrous Telephone," reflected the expectation:

> *You stay at home and listen*
> *To the lecture in the hall,*
> *Or hear the strains of music*
> *From a fashionable ball!*

Such ideas received decreasing emphasis as the telephone became largely—and very profitably—a vehicle for two-way talk. Still, as late as 1890, the magazine *Electrical Engineer* was chiding the American Telephone and Telegraph Company for not pursuing the idea of "furnishing of musical and other entertainments by wire at the fireside." Enthusiasts within AT&T likewise plumped for the idea.

The invention of wireless a few years later gave the notion new life. Guglielmo Marconi, its principal inventor, was interested in it chiefly as a device for messages, such as ship-to-shore messages, sent via code; but other experimenters shifted the attention to transmission of speech and music. Among these was a Canadian, Reginald Fessenden. Experimenting at Brant Rock, Massachusetts, on Christmas Eve of 1906, he created excitement on many ships in the North Atlantic. Wireless operators with earphones clamped to their heads, alert for the crackle of dots and dashes, were amazed to hear, instead, a woman singing, a man reading a Bible passage, and a violin solo. The solo was by Fessenden himself, playing Gounod's "O Holy Night"; he also contributed the Bible reading. The woman's voice came from a phonograph record.

The program was heard by ships as far away as the Caribbean—and perhaps caused even more astonishment than a Christmas Eve broadcast relayed years later by a far more sophisticated music machine—the 1968 moon-orbiting spaceship, Apollo 8.

The excitement stirred by Fessenden was fanned with missionary zeal by the inventor Lee De Forest. His work seemed to be inspired by the dream of "broadcasting" music far and wide. The dream found frequent expression in his diary, written in a somewhat archaic prose style. While working for the telephone company in Chicago, he conducted radio experiments in his rented room and on rooftops, and wrote in his diary:

> *What finer task than to transfer the sound of a voice of song to one a thousand miles away? If I could do that tonight!*

After patenting his Audion tube in 1906—probably the most crucial development in electronics history—he began demonstrations in New York. On March 5, 1907, he wrote in his diary:

> *My present task (happy one) is to distribute sweet music broadcast over the city and sea so that even the mariner far·out across the silent waves may hear the music of his homeland.* . . . .

De Forest went in for sensational stunts to promote the broadcasting of music. In 1908 he broadcast phonograph records from the Eiffel Tower; in 1910, the voice of Enrico Caruso "live" from the stage of the Metropolitan Opera House; in 1916, from De Forest's laboratory, the young singer Vaughn De Leath, who thus acquired the title, "the radio girl." A scattering of enthusiasts heard these broadcasts and were duly amazed, in spite of technical problems. Reporting the Caruso broadcast, the *New York Times* described the "homeless song waves" as constantly losing their way; nevertheless, said one listener, you could "catch the ecstasy."

Thousands of radio amateurs were by now emulating De Forest and entertaining each other with talk and music, live or recorded. All of this was stopped by American entry into World War I, when the federal government ruled the activity off the air in favor of military priorities. Radio now came to be thought of as an instrument for spies, rescue missions, and the coordination of battle maneuvers. Major corporations like General Electric, Westinghouse, and AT&T (via its Western Electric subsidiary) went into mass production to supply radio equipment for our armed forces. Technical advances were made, notably by Edwin H. Armstrong, who devised spectacular new circuits for the Signal Corps. Amid military pressures, music was almost forgotten.

But the sudden end of war orders in 1919 brought an industrial crisis, which set the stage for a dramatic return to the idea of broadcasting music and other entertainment. Westinghouse had been making, for army use, receiving sets that were comparatively easy to operate. The company wondered whether the general public might be persuaded to buy such sets. In 1920, to promote the notion, Westinghouse launched station KDKA, Pittsburgh, promising set owners a continuing service. It followed with WJZ, Newark; WBZ, Springfield (Massachusetts); KYW, Chicago—all launched with the same pledge as inducement to set-buyers. The strategy created a set-buying stampede, and caused innumerable companies to jump on the radio bandwagon as set-makers or broadcasters or both. Among them was General Electric. Along with Westinghouse, it at first marketed its receiving sets through the Radio Corporation of America, a new company which GE and Westinghouse and AT&T jointly controlled. RCA had originally been formed to provide an international message service, but its commercial manager, David Sarnoff, was an ardent proponent of the "radio music box" idea, and pushed the company into a leading role in the new field.

The impact of radio on musical tastes and consumption patterns was far-reaching but full of contradictions. As musical artists—along with comedians, orators, and others—flocked to the new stations to volunteer their services, the stations began to aspire to an aura of Culture. Live "radio concerts" became frequent, introduced by announcers in tuxedoes and stiff shirts. Some stations called their studios "conservatories." The favored music was light classical or quasi-classical; one observer called it "potted-palm music." In many cities, hotels acquired radio stations, and nothing was more natural than to use the string quartets that entertained unobtrusively at tea and dinner; such music became a radio staple. Organ music from theaters and department stores (the Wanamaker stores had for some time offered their customers organ recitals) became another radio favorite.

Focusing on such symbols of Culture, most broadcasters of the early 1920s shunned both jazz and country music, which were felt to have no place in a refined atmosphere. Stations that experimented with jazz—WBBM, Chicago, was one of them—were severely criticized for desecrating the air.

Ironically, this was the period when jazz was having its most explosive growth. The fact that early radio ignored jazz may have saved the phonograph industry. Many observers considered the phonograph doomed because the advent of radio brought a catastrophic drop in the sale of discs—except in one category, the so-called "race" records. Sold through separate catalogs—at first, mainly in black ghettos—the records of artists like Bessie Smith continued to have a boom sale. Bessie Smith records apparently kept Columbia Records afloat, and Victor and Brunswick likewise began to emphasize their "race" products. While this meant salvation for the companies, it also provided Negro jazz with a voice that eventually gave it wide influence, changing radio itself.

At first the influence was indirect, and came through artists like Bing Crosby and Hoagy Carmichael whose radio successes were built on styles derived from avid study of jazz recordings. The discs became texts for a rising generation of musicians. The music of orchestra leaders like Vincent Lopez and Paul Whiteman reflected the influence, though tempered with traditional orchestrations. Jazz thus swept into radio in decaffeinated form; gradually, Negro artists followed. By the 1930s jazz—black and white—was a principal radio staple.

Country music went through a somewhat similar cycle. It too began to play a strong role in the resurgence of phonograph records; these created stars who then became regional and national radio favorites. This development made WSM, Nashville, a national country-music center.

While radio moved in one direction toward popular jazz and country music, it moved in another direction toward increasingly ambitious operatic and symphonic music, which had its climax in the NBC Symphony Orchestra conducted by Arturo Toscanini. The influence of this orchestra and of the CBS-New York Philharmonic broadcasts in widening the audience for classical music has long been recognized. The LP record and FM radio have been important forces in carrying on this tradition.

Those who can now take for granted the extraordinary fidelity of FM stereo broadcasting may find it difficult to imagine the impact of a moment in 1935 when Edwin Armstrong demonstrated FM at a meeting of the Institute of Radio Engineers. First, as the receiver groped through the void, the assembled group heard a sound that FM listeners would come to know, resembling the roar of surf. Then, as the experimental FM station was tuned in, came an unearthly silence, as though the set had suddenly gone off; then, words and sounds of supernatural clarity. The pouring of water sounded liquid and not, as in AM, like a scraping fender. As for music, the engineers were suddenly aware of all that they had never heard on radio. Thus FM opened a new musical era—yet not without struggle. David Sarnoff described FM as not just an invention but "a revolution," and many saw it as a danger to other interests. And its advent did—like the advent of AM radio earlier—bring an adjustment in the roles of various media.

Only a few years later, the coming of television did precisely the same. Radio, phonograph, and films all felt overwhelmed by the new machine, and all sought to evolve new roles for themselves. Radio became mainly dependent on phonograph records and made stars of its disc jockeys. As television became the "establishment" medium, radio and its disc jockeys paid increasing attention to various minority interests such as black culture and youth culture—often conveying in their music an anti-establishment orientation. Once more, behind struggles between media and musical genres, lay social struggles and tensions. Today our music machines—American style—operate in the midst of such tensions. All this helps to make the study of music machines and their role in our lives a subject of absorbing interest to social historians.

IRVING KOLODIN ON RECORDING

For those who have passed or are approaching the threshold of fifty, every collection of objects related to the past brings back the sights with which one grew up, the look and shape of bygone times.

"The History of Music Machines" is special, even unique, because it adds, to the sights and shapes, the *sounds* of times now gradually and sometimes precipitously becoming remote. But the sound is enduring for all that. However dated the purpose and function of such an invention as the player piano or the hand-operated phonograph, the popular tune it projected is, or may still be, a part of contemporary life. "There Are Smiles That Make You Happy" was, in 1922, an invitation to euphoria extended by the parted lips of one's beloved. Fifty years later, the euphoria, as well as the beloved, may have vanished from memory, but the song's invitation persists.

It persists in more than small measure because of one or another of these music machines, which range from the simple and rudimentary to the grandiose and complex. Each expresses, through the ingenuity and determination of an inventor, a desire to make the moment immortal and the transitory permanent.

Some had antecedents and a few have had offspring. If today's compact, remarkably versatile cassette seems utterly unrelated to day-before-yesterday's 78-rpm shellac disc, it may be because few of us are versed in such matters as the laws of motion, the conversion of one form of physical or mechanical energy into another—even less in how sound becomes an electric impulse that can be sent over long distances and converted to sound again. To many of us, the kinship between the squiggles a cutting head leaves on a wax surface and the invisible rearrangements of molecules on a ferrous oxide tape must simply be taken on faith. Beyond everything else, what they have in common is a stored content to be reactivated at the convenience of the user, wherever he may be and whenever the urge possesses him.

It is of abiding interest that two distinct purposes have prevailed, however the means have been transformed over decades. One is to perpetuate the vast variety of auditory experiences available at any particular time. This may range from the voice of Enrico Caruso to that of Al Jolson, from the former's vibrant (if phonetic) pronouncement "Over There" at a Wall Street bond-selling rally **13** at the height of World War I to the latter's exuberant "April Showers" in the early twenties. By then the Great War was receding into the past, and the most important thought of millions was what happened after April showers came "allahhahong" ("they bring the flowers that bloom in May").

The other purpose is the harnessing of mechanical means to create new sounds unimaginable without them. These could encompass not only the Stroh violin, an offshoot of early recording techniques in which the noble shape perfected by Stradivarius was bastardized by the subtraction of the back and belly and the substitution of a small horn that would feed vibrations onto waiting wax, but also the orchestrion, a huge evolution out of the player piano.

From the development of the vacuum tube that made radio possible came Leon Theremin's quavery tone generator, later the Ondes Martinot and, more recently, the Moog and Putney synthesizers which can produce combinations of sounds wholly beyond the capacity of conventional instruments or even that most remarkable instrument of them all, the human voice.

That there are still people who make music with that amazingly versatile sound box which is everyone's birthright is proof that, however much inventive genius flourishes, simple basic impulses cannot be expunged from the human psyche. It may surprise younger readers that some not yet of Social Security age recall a time when the springs that caused a turntable to revolve were wound by a crank before every record; and when player pianos were activated by bellows pumped by foot. So great a music critic as Ernest Newman wrote a book on how to play the player piano. It was his thesis that if the user understood such terms as accelerando and rubato, pianissimo and fortissimo, the book would make a participant of a consumer and enable thousands who hadn't the patience to practice to be proficient player-pianists. I do not think it was among his most flourishing publications.

The first conversion of a human function to a mechanical one *vis-a-vis* the phonograph came, as I recall, with the introduction of a device by which a spring motor could be electrically wound. A metal case about the size of a hand grenade was plugged into the hole that accommodated the crank handle. When the electric outlet was connected, and a button depressed, the winding shaft revolved. Result: a well-wound spring motor in a fraction of the time required to rewind the spring by hand. In the later twenties there was an all-electric phonograph called the Cheney which did everything admirably: revolve the turntable, pick up the sound, deliver it in some semblance of quality. The only weak link in the chain was an inadequate motor, whose bearings overheated under extended use. When they "froze" and the turntable stopped revolving, everything admirable about the Cheney might as well not have existed.

Curiously, for all the impulse provided to sound reproduction through development of the vacuum tube, amplifiers, and primitive loudspeakers, the motor continued to be the vulnerable point in the potential giant's makeup. An effort to extend the playing time of the twelve-inch disc beyond its long-established limit of four minutes came to a disastrous end during demonstrations in 1931. Presumably the monster had been docile enough in the laboratory, but the unsteady revolutions of an inadequately engineered motor—for the critical speed of 33⅓ revolutions per minute—left musicians unhappy and the sponsors nonplussed.

This was, in a way, an exquisite form of technological justice. Even had all gone well, the thick shellac disc and the grinding surface noise produced by a metal stylus would have limited its use to those addicted to progress at whatever cost. Not until wartime (1941) shortages of shellac (a commodity out of Burma that was early cut off from the Western world) brought about the development of a vinyl disc—light, unbreakable, and suitable for shipment to army personnel all over the world—was the beginning of a revolution in sight.

Coupled with the slower speed AND a narrower (micro) groove that extended playing time six- or sevenfold was a diamond-tipped stylus and a dependable motor. For the first time in phonographic history, the discriminating public was offered a product in which each element had been tailored to the other, including a pickup whose pressure was measured in grams rather than ounces. When it was finally mated with Full Frequency Range Reproduction (London Decca's FFRR by-product of a listening device keen enough to enable its operator to distinguish a German sub's engines from ours), the means for a wholly integrated *system* were finally at hand.

Anything introduced since then, whether additional channels, more sound dispersers, headphones, etc., has merely been a refinement of the basic 33⅓ revolution and nothing inherently new in itself. Even tape, with its quality possibilities (and built-in limitations) is, in effect, no more than a groove wrapped around a reel rather than spread out flat on a disc. Some may quarrel with this description, but tape does trade some of its advantages in lightness and compactness for the accessibility of any point on a disc.

Over the years, the debates have continued about the pros and cons of music machines, the impact of their existence on the habit patterns of society, the extent to which they supplement or replace live participation in music making, their influence for good or evil on taste. Certainly they have tended to make a sedentary society even more sedentary by discouraging not merely the winding of a motor but the replacement of a record that has been playing for nearly half an hour.

As for taste, it has been driven to the wall, and all but through it, by exploitation of the music machines' potential for serving the lowest common denominator. Whether in records, or in radio's reliance on the Top Forty—those loudest, hardest, often cheapest appeals to the beetle-browed—selectivity has long since foundered on the rock of commercialism. There are sections of the country through which one can drive for days without hearing anything on the radio other than Nashville, country, or down home.

Somehow, though, in spite of all the music machines' seduction of the sedentary, promotion of the commonplace, and exploitation of the path of least resistance, the elite music schools—Juilliard, Curtis, Eastman—find themselves under siege from increasing numbers of applicants. Someone out there is listening to something other than rock or pop—and is getting something out of it.

The gist of the matter is: what are music machines asked to do, however they look or however much they cost? Properly used, an inexpensive record player —serviced with a discriminating cross section of the thousands of long-playing records created in the last two decades—can facilitate research, foster knowledge, and promote musical understanding in ways unimaginable to our fathers, let alone our forefathers. Casually or thoughtlessly used, a music machine can disrupt the peace, disturb domestic tranquility, and infest a neighborhood as surely as a spilled test tube of bacteria can create an epidemic.

Music machines, like computers, are devices to implement man's purposes, not to determine them. As no computer can proceed from information to wisdom, so no music machine can ennoble, aggrandize, or even prettify, the use to which it is put by its master. Music machines make marvelous servants but debilitating masters.

THE
HISTORY
OF
MUSIC
MACHINES

The alliance of music and science has brought about revolutionary changes in the performance, reproduction, and dissemination of music in America.

With the development of the phonograph, player piano, radio, movie, and tape machine, music not only became immediately available to a world audience but could be recorded for later study and enjoyment. Electronic instruments have provided an unlimited source of new sounds.

Americans have always shown a need for music in their daily lives for worship, for cultural enrichment, for entertainment. At various times, this need could be satisfied by touring concert artists, local bands and choirs, traveling minstrel shows, and the piano in the parlor. But when talent was lacking and the touring musicians had moved on, Americans turned increasingly to machines for their music.

"The History of Music Machines" is a three-dimensional chronology not only of the music and machines that originated in the United States but also of imports that were absorbed—and often transformed—by Americans.

MUSIC   "Excelsior" (mazurka)—Masenco
         "Gasparoune" (polka)—Karl Millöcker
         Pinned cylinder; music box,
         about 1890.

         "Watch on the Rhine"—Carl Friedrich Wilhelm
         "Tramp, Tramp, Tramp"—George Frederick Root
         Paper roll; Clariona reed organ, 1882.

         "Yankee Doodle"—anonymous
         Pinned cylinder; Hicks barrel organ, about 1860.

MUSIC AND MACHINES IN THE 19th CENTURY

Many Americans applied muscle power to the cranks of new mechanical instruments to provide music when "live" talent was unavailable.

Madame Marie Rôze with an Edison tinfoil cylinder phonograph. Cover of Frank Leslie's Illustrated Newspaper, April 20, 1878.

BARREL ORGAN

Equipped with such tunes as "Yankee Doodle" and a duet from the opera *Norma*, barrel organs provided mechanical music at outdoor gatherings.

A player turns the crank; this pumps the bellows and rotates the barrel (or wooden cylinder) on which metal staples or pins are inserted. The pins activate a mechanism that causes the pipes to play the selected tune.

Barrel organ, mid-19th century. Made by George Hicks, Brooklyn, New York. Gift of Hugo Worch. Catalog number 299,855 (Lautman photo 77362.)

From Frank Leslie's Illustrated Newspaper, *January 12, 1878.*

NEW YORK CITY.—THE MEMBERS OF THE STOCK EXCHANGE INDULGING IN A HOLIDAY FROLIC ON THE DAY BEFORE CHRISTMAS.—See Page 273.

Detail of the Hicks barrel organ showing the pins on the barrel and the wooden pipes. Catalog number 299,855. (Lautman photo 77378.)

Unidentified organ grinder, late 19th century. From Library of Congress.

Edison cylinder machine with the tinfoil partially recorded, 1878. Made by Brehmer Brothers, Philadelphia. Gift of Princeton University. Catalog number 318,576. (Lautman photo 77200.)

Edison machine showing the grooves on the cylinder that help to direct the cutting stylus. Catalog number 318,576. (77135A.)

From Harper's Weekly, *March 30, 1878.*

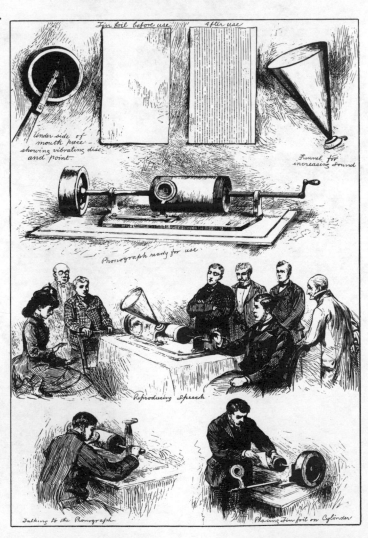

EDISON'S SPEAKING PHONOGRAPH

"IT TALKS. IT WHISPERS. IT SINGS." So announced an advertisement of the remarkable 1877 invention of Thomas A. Edison. For two dollars, a home could be equipped with a machine that recorded and reproduced the human voice.

Though miraculous, the sounds reproduced by cranking these crude tinfoil cylinder machines were parodies of the original. Edison's prediction that his invention would benefit business, family, music, and education did not seem possible until he began to improve his phonograph about a decade later.

Cover of "The Song of Mister Phonograph," 1878.

CYLINDER MUSIC BOX

Swiss music boxes of the late 19th century were among the earliest types of mechanical instruments for the home. A tune is played by winding a crank, which causes the metal cylinder to rotate. The delicate sounds thus produced by pins plucking the metal comb were sometimes accompanied by bells and drum.

These music boxes were expensive, however, and many were limited to only a few tunes. By the early 20th century, most home listeners preferred disc music boxes and talking machines that overcame both these limitations.

Cylinder music box, about 1890. Made by Mermod Fréres, Sainte-Croix, Switzerland. Gift of August Mencken. Catalog number 69.20. (77141B.)

Detail of an imported music box. Catalog number 69.20. (Lautman photo 77377.)

Music-box dealers even sold songs written about their wares, such as "Recollections of a Music Box," 1875. From Warshaw Collection of Business Americana, Smithsonian Institution.

The Berliner Gramophone, 1893.
Made by U.S. Gramophone Co.,
Washington, D. C. Gift of
Emile Berliner. Catalog number
307,204. (Lautman photo
77201.)

BERLINER GRAMOPHONE

The early disc talking machine, a gramophone patented by Emile Berliner in 1887, required an operator with patience and a strong and steady arm. To play a record, it was necessary to crank furiously on the handle until the turntable was revolving about seventy times a minute. Keeping that speed constant, the operator then set the needle on the record with his free hand.

With each machine, the manufacturer offered this thoughtful advice: "Don't get discouraged if the machine doesn't give entire satisfaction *at once.* It will take a *little practice . . .*"

Rear view of Berliner Gramophone. Catalog number 307,204. (77140.)

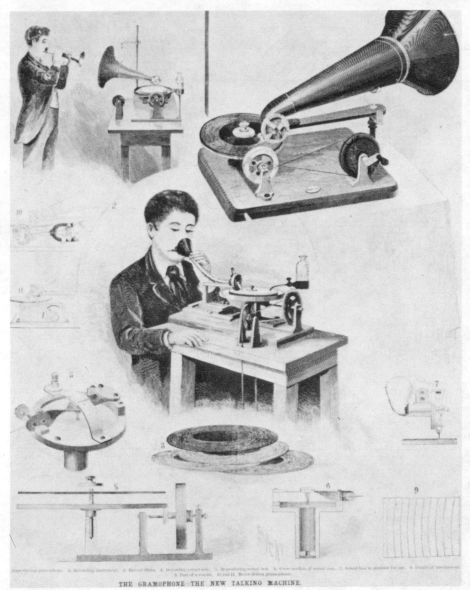

THE GRAMOPHONE—THE NEW TALKING MACHINE.

Title page from Scientific American, *May 16, 1896.*

From an instruction book for the Gramophone, about 1895.

The Clariona, 1882. Made in New York. Gift of J. Howard Foote. Catalog number 72,881. (Lautman photo 77193.)

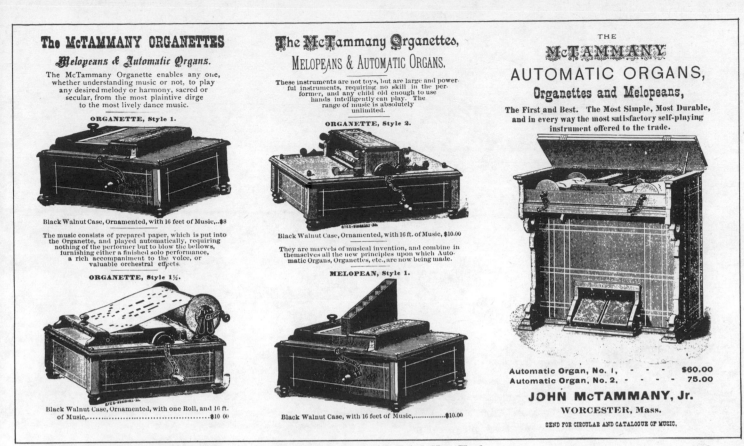

Advertisement of hand-cranked reed organs. From archive of Frederick Fried, New York.

CLARIONA

Basically a small reed organ, the Clariona was one of the first mechanical instruments to use a perforated paper roll. When pumped by the crank, the bellows provide air to activate the reeds.

Its promoters claimed that this was no "trashy toy," but a "GENUINE MUSICAL INSTRUMENT . . . with the carrying quality of a large pipe organ," good for sustained sacred music or the largest dance halls.

MUSIC   "Semper Fidelis"—John Philip Sousa
Acoustic recording; Sousa's Band, 1908; Victor 16190.

"No One but You Know How to Love Me"
Jo' Trent-Allen-Peter De Rose-Allan Frazer-May Singhi Breen
Paper roll, 1926; Violano-Virtuoso, player piano, violin, 1914.

"Love is a Tyrant" from *The Singing Girl*—Harry B. Smith,
Victor Herbert.
"Listen to the Mocking Bird"—Alice Hawthorne, Richard Milburn.
Metal disc; Regina disc-changer, about 1900.

MUSIC PARLORS—PUBLIC AND PRIVATE

Improved talking machines and their
competitors were entertaining thousands of
Americans by the 1890s at phonograph
parlors, penny arcades, and concert
exhibitions of the phonograph, as well as
at social functions in the home.

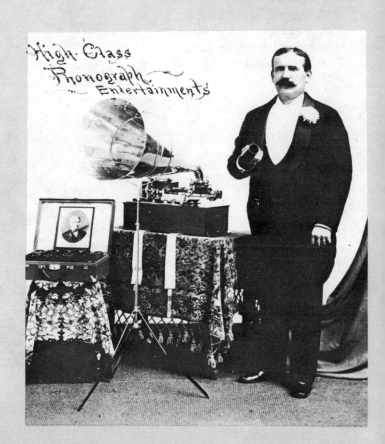

*Publicity for cylinder-machine concert exhibition, 1890s.
From Library of Congress.*

EDISON AUTOMATIC PHONOGRAPH

Such performances as Sousa's band playing "The Stars and Stripes Forever" or the Haydn Male Quartet singing "Nearer My God to Thee" could be heard in the 1890s on the Edison Automatic Phonograph for a nickel a tune at public exhibition parlors—or at drugstores and beer gardens. Patrons listened through earphones.

Edison Automatic Phonograph, 1897. Made by North American Phonograph Co., New York. Gift of Oliver Read. Catalog number 324,168. (Lautman photo 77349.)

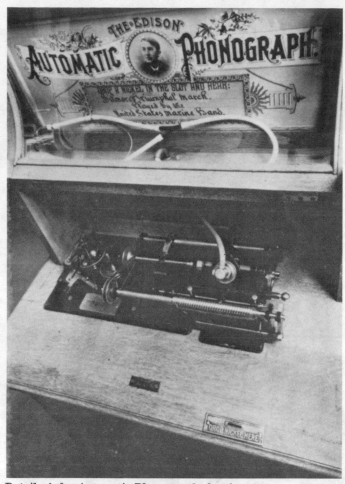

Detail of the Automatic Phonograph showing the mechanism and coin slot. Catalog number 324,168. (Lautman photo 77375.)

Man listening to the Edison Automatic Phonograph. From The Phonogram, *February 1891.*

Peter Bacigalupi's Kinetoscope, Phonograph, and Graphophone Arcade in San Francisco around 1900. Note the linen napkins provided to clean the earphones.

MULTIPHONE

The first selective coin-operated phonograph, this early version of the jukebox held twenty-four cylinders as compared with one available on the Edison Automatic. To hear a tune from among those listed on the title chart, the listener deposited his nickel, turned the selector crank until his desired cylinder reached playing position, and then supplied the power himself by turning the spring motor crank.

The Multiphone, 1905-08. Made by Multiphone Operating Co., New York. Gift of Oliver Read. Catalog number 324,141. (Lautman photo 77364.)

Detail of the Multiphone showing its intricate mechanism. Catalog number 324,141. (Lautman photo 77365.)

REGINA HEXAPHONE

The Regina phonograph, introduced in 1908, offered patrons the choice of six 4-minute cylinders. At the drop of a nickel and a few turns of the crank, the latest songs were available through the well-designed enclosed wooden horn.

The Regina Hexaphone, made about 1909 by Regina Co., New York. Gift of Oliver Read. Catalog number 324,142. (Lautman photo 77188.)

Detail of the mechanism of the Regina Hexaphone. Catalog number 324,142. (Lautman photo 77189.)

Cover of an advertising booklet for the Regina Hexaphone. From archive of Frederick Fried, New York.

Detail of the tune indicator on the Regina Hexaphone. Catalog number 324,142. (Lautman photo 77190.)

VIOLANO-VIRTUOSO

First manufactured in 1909, the
Violano-Virtuoso is a self-playing
combination violin-piano that was
popular in homes, restaurants, clubs,
and resorts until the late 1920s.
Powered by electricity, it plays paper
music rolls. Selections ranged from
popular tunes to such classics as
Beethoven's Violin Concerto, a *tour
de force* for the mechanical violin.

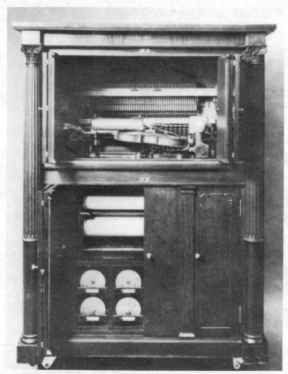

*Violano-Virtuoso made especially for the
Smithsonian Institution in 1914, by Mills Novelty
Co., Chicago. Catalog number 283,285.
(Lautman photo 77366.)*

*View of Violano-Virtuoso paper roll in place.
Holes on the right of the paper roll activate
the mechanism for the mechanical violin; those
on the left, the piano. Catalog number 283,285.
(Lautman photo 77367.)*

Detail of violin mechanism. The metal fingers that reach up to stop the violin strings vividly depict the replacement of man by a machine. Catalog number 283,285. (Lautman photo 77367.)

Advertisement from the Violano-Virtuoso Handbook, *about 1910.*

The Children's Party

"The reason that boys and girls leave home," once said a keen observer, "is that so few homes are made interesting for young people. The natural craving for amusement very often overcomes personal attachments."

Will you admit that you cannot give your children better reason to pass their evenings with you than to seek elsewhere for an outlet for youthful spirits? If you have sought for means to make your home attractive and have failed to solve the problem, why not get a Violano-Virtuoso? With it you can provide a source of constant interest and enjoyment.

And there is still another important reason why you should have this instrument—it will develop the finer instincts in minds which are most receptive to influence. It will cultivate perceptions and create and enlarge ideals which might otherwise never become matured.

You can buy a piano or a violin, but consider that it will be years before a child can play either of them well, and then only if practice has been a daily duty constantly performed. Why should you spend the money for music lessons, and why should the satisfaction of enjoying the best playing of the best compositions be deferred when you can have a Violano-Virtuoso now?

Look back upon your own childhood and think what it would have meant to you then if you could have had such a means of recreation. Consider how satisfying it would have been for you to learn while still young, all the fine points of musical literature? Do you know them even now?

If you had to sacrifice the advantages given by the Violano-Virtuoso, see that your children have them.

Regina Disc Changer. Made about 1900 by Regina Musical Box Co., Rahway, New Jersey. Lent by Edwin Pugsley. (Lautman photo 77195.)

Detail of Regina Disc Changer. (Lautman photo 77196.)

REGINA DISC CHANGER

To compete with early cylinder phonographs, manufacturers of disc music boxes developed a 2-minute metal disc that played many of the same operatic and popular tunes on its seven-octave metal comb. Fitted with an automatic tune-changing device that allowed twelve tunes to be played at one winding, these machines have a beautiful tonal quality that made them popular.

The small disc music boxes, unable to match the popularity of the talking machines, were even manufactured in a combination model, as this early 20th-century advertisement shows. From Warshaw Collection of Business Americana, Smithsonian Institution.

Concert phonograph exhibition kits were advertised in mail-order catalogs of the late 1890s for public entertainments in halls and churches as well as for home amusement. And it is to the home trade that talking-machine manufacturers turned their attention as they developed the inexpensive models found in many households before the turn of the century.

The Sears catalog of 1898 offered for sale the Graphophone, a cylinder machine patented by Alexander Graham Bell, Chichester Bell, and Charles Sumner Tainter in 1886. Along with the concert-exhibition machine, one could buy posters, tickets, and a small printing outfit to change the date and location on the posters. From Warshaw Collection of Business Americana, Smithsonian Institution.

42

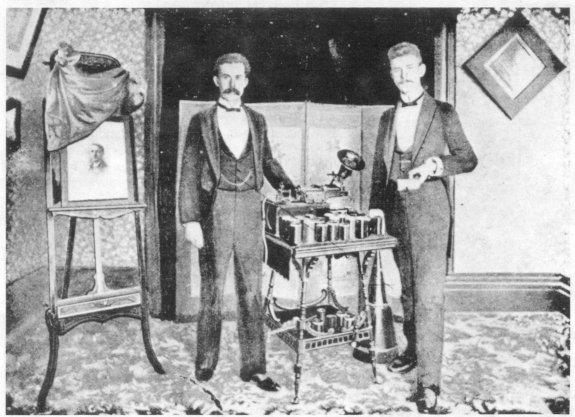

The Sullivan brothers, who wrote the article "How to Give Concert Exhibitions of the Phonograph." From The Phonogram, *February 1893.*

A group listening to the phonograph at Smith Brothers, Poughkeepsie, New York. From The Phonogram, *March-April 1893.*

EDISON GEM PHONOGRAPH
COLUMBIA EAGLE GRAPHOPHONE

These simple, inexpensive machines brought recorded sound into the home. Although the Edison Gem was capable only of playing records, its low price of $7.50 made it popular.

The Columbia Eagle and all other Edison home models were also equipped with a recording diaphragm, which provided the proud owner with the means to record and preserve the sounds of his child's voice or the music-making of his family and friends.

Edison Gem Phonograph. Made in 1912 by National Phonograph Co., New York.
Gift of Oliver Read. Catalog number 324,177. (77141.)

The Columbia Eagle Graphophone was one of many home machines mounted on compact carrying cases quite similar to those of sewing machines. Made in 1899 by American Graphophone Co., New York. Gift of Mrs. Carrie M. Orum Spawn. Catalog number 312,019. (Lautman photo 77350.)

Detail of recording stylus of the Columbia Eagle Graphophone. Catalog number 312,019. (Lautman photo 77351.)

Improved Berliner Gramophone with spring-wound motor, about 1899. Made by National Gramophone Co., New York. Gift of Oliver Read. Catalog number 324,164. (Lautman photo 77199.)

BERLINER GRAMOPHONE

The improved Berliner Gramophone became a serious competitor to the cylinder trade after it was fitted in 1896 with a springwound motor developed by Eldridge Johnson, who later founded the Victor Talking Machine Company. Its disc record was easier than a cylinder to play, store, and duplicate—factors that led to its great popularity soon after the turn of the century.

The famous Victor trademark shows Nipper, the dog, listening to a similar machine.

LIST OF PLATES.

JANUARY 1895.

BAND MUSIC.

118 Dude's March
130 Black and Tan
111 Marching Through Georgia, (with cheers)
111 The same—Patrol
  2 La Serenata
115 Star Spangled Banner
  8 Coxey's Army
 11 Salvation Army
  9 Semper Fidelis (with drums.)
139 After the Ball
126 Bocaccio March
144 Liberty Bell March
140 Washington Post March
142 Admirals Favorite March
  4 Friedensklange
105 National Fencibles
 13 Gladiator March
 19 Schottische, Nancy Hanks
 15 Loin du bal
 17 Waltz, Aphrodite
 20 Mendelsohn's Wedding March

INSTRUMENTAL QUARTETTE.

807 Die Kapelle
803 Circus Band
806 March, King John
800 Ein neues Blatt

BARYTONE.

163 When Summer Comes Again
182 Sweetheart Nell, and I
175 Old Kentucky Home
191 Black Knight Templars
185 Throw Him Down McCloskey
183 Oh, Promise Me
176 Love Me Little, Love Me Long
150 Oh, Fair Art Thou
155 Anchored
170 Mamie Come Kiss your Honey Boy
166 Then You'll Remember Me
160 The Maiden and the Lamb
165 Red, White and Blue
169 The Coon That Got the Shake
157 Tramp, Tramp, Tramp
158 Sweet Marie
196 The Whistling Coon
189 Phœbe
193 Back among the old folks
198 Swim out O'Grady
902 Sword of Bunker Hill

CLARIONET.

300 Allegro (Verdi)

CORNET.

200 Polka, Elegant
205 Call Me Thy Own
206 Emily Polka
202 U. S. Military Signals
203 Welcome, Pretty Primrose

Cornet Continued.

211 Cloverleaf Polka

CORNET DUETTS.

242 Alpine Polka
248 Swiss Boy
243 La Paloma

DRUM AND FIFE.

700 Biddy Oates
706 American Medley
702 St. Patrick's day
705 The Spirit of '76 (very dramatic)

TROMBONE.

75 In The Deep Cellar

PIANO.

256 Geisterfunken
253 March, Jolly Minstrels

INDIAN SONGS.

51 Three Melodies from the Ghost Dance
52 Three Melodies from the Ghost Dance
50 Three Melodies from the Ghost Dance

ANIMALS.

53 Morning on the farm

Hebrew Melodies.

400 Parshe Zav

SOPRANO.

359 Oh, Promise Me
352 Oh, How Delightful
355 Star Spangled Banner
353 I've something sweet to tell you
363 Tell her I love her so
362 Some Day
350 Past and Future
365 Punchinello
354 In the gloaming
356 Loves Sorrow

CONTRALTO.

550 Beauties Eyes
551 Drink to me only
552 Oh, Promise me

RECITATION.

We have for this important department secured the co-operation of the eminent, versatile elocutionist, **Mr. David C. Bangs.**
602 Marc Anthony's Curse
      A Lesson in Elocution.
600 The Village Blacksmith
      (Many others in preparation.)

VOCAL QUARTETTE.

851 Blind Tom (negro shout)
853 Grandfather's Birthday
855 Negroes' holiday

It is expected that between 25 and 50 New Pieces will be added every month.

THE UNITED STATES GRAMOPHONE CO.,
1410 Pennsylvania Ave., N. W.,
Washington, D. C.

1895 list of Gramophone plates.

The Victor stained-glass window, 1915. Gift of RCA.
Catalog number 330,390. (Lauman photo 77369.)

STAINED-GLASS WINDOW

One of four installed in the Victor tower in 1915,
the window depicting the familiar Victor trademark, Nipper listening to His Master's Voice, was
a famous landmark in Camden, New Jersey,
until 1969.

Victor tower in Camden, New Jersey; windows designed by Philadelphia artist Nicola D'Ascenzo (who also designed windows for the National Cathedral, Washington, D. C., and the Cathedral of St. John The Divine, New York).

The Victrola IV with the enclosed horn. 1907 model made by Victor Talking Machine Co., Camden, New Jersey. Gift of Oliver Read. Catalog number 324,206. (Lautman photo 77192.)

VICTROLA IV

The Victrola, a talking machine designed with an internal horn, became available in 1906. No longer was it necessary, Victor salesmen claimed, to display in the parlor an object resembling a sewing machine with an oversized horn.

Although some listeners maintained that open-horn machines produced a better sound, the Victrola soon became a common household possession and a generic name for all talking machines.

GIVEN AWAY ABSOLUTELY FREE

Latest Type Hornless Talking Machine

This Most Wonderful Home Entertainer One to Every Family in this Locality

Gives Joy—Pleasure—Anywhere—Everywhere !

 F R E E

At This Store Only to Our Customers

 F R E E

How to Get One of These Machines Free with $25 Cash Trade

These Machines are given away to ADVERTISE A WELL-KNOWN DISC TALKING MACHINE RECORD. The manufacturers are of the opinion that if several hundred of their machines were placed in that many homes in this vicinity, it would create an enormous demand for their Records.

The instruments are now on display in our windows. Call and see them.

YOU DON'T PAY ONE SINGLE PENNY FOR THIS MACHINE.

Commencing this date a free talking machine coupon will be given with every purchase, according to the amount of your sale. For example: If your purchase amounts to $2.50, you will receive coupons to that amount. You save these; when you have a total amounting to $25.00 worth of coupons, BRING THEM IN AND EXCHANGE THEM FOR A TALKING MACHINE ABSOLUTELY FREE.

THE FAIR DEP'T. STORE :: Lakeview, Ill.

Advertisement for a hornless talking machine. From Warshaw Collection of Business Americana, Smithsonian Institution.

MUSIC   "I Ain't Givin' Nothin' Away"—Louis E. Zoeller
James P. Johnson; player-piano roll, 1921.
RCA Victor LSP-2058

"Mes Longs Cheveux" from *Pélleas et Mélisande*—
Claude Debussy
Mary Garden, soprano; Claude Debussy, piano.
Edison Pathé acoustic recording, 1902;
Reissued: Everest-Scalla, 829A.

"Smiles"—J. Will Calahan, Lee S. Roberts
Lee S. Roberts and Max Kortlander; player-piano roll, 1917.
RCA Victor LSP-2058

MUSIC MACHINES IN THE HOME

In the first decade of the 20th century, the
talking machine and player piano became
widely available in both simple and elaborate
models. Thus, Americans of all economic levels
could listen, dance, and sing to the same music.

*"In Georgia—Bringing Home the Victor." From
The Victor in Rural Schools. Camden, New Jersey,
Victor Talking Machine Co., 1916.*
© *RCA Records.*

EDISON HOME PHONOGRAPH

The cylinder trade flourished in small towns and rural areas. Through morning-glory horns (and later, even larger horns) Americans from modest homes heard music described by a 1910 Edison trade publication as good old ragtime—Sousa—Herbert—monologues—sentimental ballads.

Believing in the superiority of cylinder recordings, Edison continued to produce them until he went out of the record business in 1929. But most of the public preferred disc machines and Edison gave in to this preference when he introduced his Disc Phonograph in 1913.

Edison Home Phonograph fitted with a painted morning-glory horn, a tripod to hold up the horn, and a cabinet that provides storage for 100 cylinders. 1907 model, made by National Phonograph Co., New York. Gift of Leonard G. Shoemaker. Catalog number 328,433. (Lautman photo 77357.)

This record-storage cabinet holds not only popular tunes of the day but also some home-produced cylinders that are carefully noted on the pages of a notebook tucked in one of its drawers. Catalog number 328,433. (Lautman photo 77358.)

1

1. Bellman, The - Song
2. Massa in the Cold Cold Ground
3. Our director - March
4. In the Valley of Kentucky - Song
5. Amona - Band
6. In the City of Sighs and Tears - Song
7. Violin & Flute Duet
8. Down on the Farm - Song
9. Broadway Hits - March
10. Under the Double Eagle March
11. Little Mazurka - Band
12. Tenth Regiment March - Band
13. Alway in the Way - Song
14. Pretty as a Picture - Song
15. Down were the Cotton Blossom Grow Song
16. It was the Dutch - Band
17. School days - Song
18. Cornation - Quartette
19. Camp Meeting Jubilee - Quartette
20. In the Golden Autumn Time - Song

2

21. Bell of New York March & Orchestra
22. American Eagle March - Band
23. My Own Kentucky Home - Quartette
24. The Robin Song - Duet
25. I'm wearing my Heart away for you - Song
26. Sweet Nellie Gray - Song
27. My Own wild western Rose - Song
28. Warbler Serenade - Band
29. When the Harvest moon - Song
30. Heinne - Duet
31. Jimmy & Maggie at the Hippedrone - Duet
32. Old Limerick Town - Band
33. Hello Central Give me Heaven - Song
34. Dixie Girl March - Band
35. Cornet Solo - Cornet
36. Killen Elanea - Song
37. Hurrah Boys March - Band
38. Sunshine will come again - Quartette
39. Prince of Pislen March - Orchestra
40. Mocking Bird - Sylophone

3

41 The Flower from Home sweet Home Quartette
42 The Lost Chord - Quartette
43 The Birds and the Brook. Orchestra
44 While the Convent Bells were singing Song
45 Baby Prayer - Duet
46 I love you So. Duet
47 Oh that we two were Maying Duet
48 The New Colonial March. Band
49 Sunny Southern Home Quartette
50 Home sweet Home - Mixed Quartette
51 Refuge - Mixed Quartette
52 Larboard Watch - Duet
53 When we were Boys - Duet
54 Enquier Club March Band
55 American Republican March - Band
56 Hiawatha - Orchestra
57 Since Nellie went away. Quartette
58 Angellina Duet
59 When were the Werstberger... Song
60 I wed... in the olden summer time Song

4

61 Sweet Antonette Duet
62 Old Homestead Quartette
63 Two Rubes in a Tavern Duet
64 Down the Line with Molly. Duet
65 Not because your Hair is Curly. Song
66 The Bridge Quartette
67 The Whistling Coon Song
68 Thatching... Duet
69 Where the silver Colorado wind'd way Song
70 ... out to night. Song
71 Nearer my God to thee Quartette
72 ...
73 The night Alarm - Orchestra
74 The Soldier Farewell - Quartette
75 Can't you see I'm lonely. Song
76
77
78
79
80

5
Home made Records

81 Mohawk Indians
82 New York Town Leonard
83 German Song - Mrs Kenney & Neffinger
84 Who there taping at my bedroom window
85 Beavers
86 Duet - Gerty and Bill Kenney
87 Beavers # 2 -
88 Gertie Ryan
89 Mother Neffinger - Three Leaves of Shamrock
90 May Wedding
91 Under the Old Cherry Tree
92 Duet Gerty and Bill Kenney
93 Starlight
94 Court Banner Quartette May Wedding
95
96
97
98
99
100

COLUMBIA GRAFONOLA

The upright disc machine represents the type of windup talking machine used in many American homes until as late as the 1940s. Although electric phonographs appeared in the late 1920s, the popularity of radio—followed by the Depression and World War II—delayed their introduction.

Columbia Grafonola, 1915 model. Made by Columbia Gramophone Co., New York. The only volume control is a knob on the right that opens and closes the louvers. Gift of Oliver Read. Catalog number 324,213. (Lautman photo 77353.)

Closeup of Columbia Grafonola. Catalog number 324,213. (Lautman photo 77352.)

Music for Everybody

Advertisement for Victor dealer, "Music for Everybody." From Warshaw Collection of Business Americana, Smithsonian Institution.

A player piano in use in 1940 in an old farmhouse occupied by migrants near Cedarville, New Jersey. Farm Security Administration photo by Delano, July 1940. From Library of Congress.

A player piano in use in 1925. From The Talking Machine World, *January 15, 1924.*

The Atwood Twentieth-Century Piano Loader from Villisca, Iowa, attached to a Ford runabout, provided many traveling salesmen with a convenient, persuasive means of introducing the piano into rural homes. From Warshaw Collection of Business Americana, Smithsonian Institution.

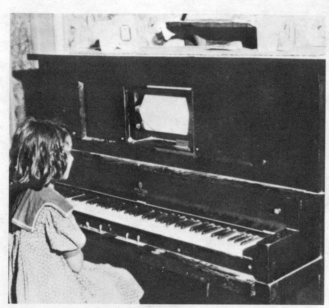

GABLER PLAYER PIANO

"A Player Piano is the Heart of a Happy Home" advised one manufacturer— and between 1900 and 1930 at least two and one-half million American homes had acquired their mechanical hearts.

The silent piano in the parlor came to life again with the addition of a pneumatic pedal-operated mechanism activated by perforated paper rolls. Recorded on the thousands of player-piano rolls were classical music, dances, popular songs, and ragtime.

REPRODUCING PLAYER PIANO

Many grand pianos were equipped with a sophisticated player mechanism that reproduced not only the notes but also the tempo, rhythm, dynamic changes, phrasing, and pedaling of the recording artist. The leading American reproducing mechanisms were Ampico and Duo Art; the imported Welte-Mignon was installed in some American pianos. This type of piano introduced many Americans to the playing of such greats as Paderewski and Gershwin and today preserves their performances better than acoustic records.

Often housed in cases of very elaborate design, reproducing pianos were found in the drawing rooms of the Astors and Vanderbilts as well as in the music departments of leading universities.

Closeup of reproducing player piano, 1928. Made by Chickering & Sons, East Rochester, New York. Fitted with Ampico mechanism.

Recording the Soul of Piano Playing

Revealing Idiosyncrasies of Artists

Pages from Ampico brochure. From Warshaw Collection of Business Americana, Smithsonian Institution.

The AMPICO in the Home

Imagine the Ampico in Your Home.

You come home from a busy day down town. You reach the seclusion of your own fireside at the twilight hour. The lamps are lighted or the glow of the fire penetrates but feebly the gathering darkness. What a moment for soft music! With the Ampico at hand one may hear any of the beautiful old songs, with their tender appeal, or the exquisite nocturnes of Chopin, or the tuneful music of Nevin or Chaminade, all ideally played.

One is in a singularly receptive mood at the day's end,

and any music heard under these conditions has a restorative influence, the reviving power of which is duly acknowledged and made use of by our scientists.

Dancing to the Ampico.

Then let us picture the family, with perhaps a young guest or two, eager for entertainment after dinner. Some one makes the happy suggestion "Let's have a dance." In a moment the rugs are rolled up, the furniture moved aside and the improvised ballroom is ready. Neighbors and acquaintances are telephoned to and in a short time the house is ringing with laughter and gaiety inseparable from the dance that *goes*. The music? Ah! the Ampico provides that, and such music, played by Broadway's masters of syncopation, irresistible in its rhythm and accent; and what is most delightful, the Ampico plays itself so that all are free to dance.

For a Musicale.

One of the most delightful afternoon entertainments is a musicale, beginning, let us say, at four o'clock. One that was actually given is charmingly described in a little pamphlet entitled "Twilight and Music." At this unusually attractive party a short program of the playing of such artists as Rachmaninoff, Godowsky, Busoni and Ornstein was offered with two groups of songs sung by a local soprano. A tastefully printed program was handed to each guest. The music lasted for one hour only, and was followed by the pleasant refreshment of afternoon tea.

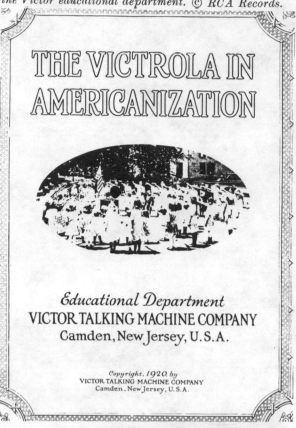

THE VICTROLA IN AMERICANIZATION

Educational Department
VICTOR TALKING MACHINE COMPANY
Camden, New Jersey, U.S.A.

Copyright, 1920, by
VICTOR TALKING MACHINE COMPANY
Camden, New Jersey, U.S.A.

Copyright 1905 by J.J. Voss, Chicago No 1

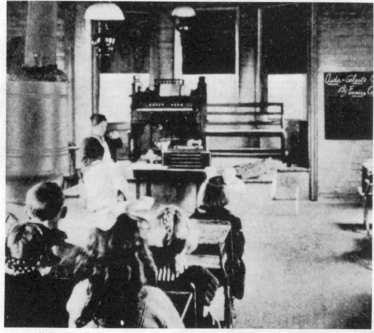

The reaction to music-reproducing machines was mixed. John Philip Sousa, composer and bandmaster, considered them a menace and in 1906 predicted "a marked deterioration in American music and musical taste" and the disappearance of the amateur musician.

But many leading musicians and music professors praised the educational value of classical records and piano rolls. Record companies published guides for classroom teachers and opera listeners, as well as dance and exercise-instruction books. Field researchers used cylinder machines to record the music and speech of American Indians.

The music machines also introduced listeners to the unique sounds of jazz and enabled musicians in remote areas and in Europe to study the styles and techniques of leading jazz players.

"Will the infant be put to sleep by machinery?"

PERTINENT POINTERS IN COUNTY INSTITUTE WORK WITH THE VICTROLA

1—The old-time story-telling, laugh-raising, barn-storming methods of institute music have no place in the modern, serious, but delightful, service of music in education.

2—Be prepared. Have a definite plan for each lesson and the whole number arranged in sequence.

3—*Start* from a given point, *proceed* in an orderly manner in a definite direction, and *arrive* at the desired goal.

4—See that the Victrola is in place *before* the opening of the session—needle set, motor wound up and ready. (Read *Rural Booklet*, page 19.) Use community band records for assembly or chapel.

5—Have the records for the lesson out of their envelopes, arranged in order on the front shelf of the instrument. After using each record place it on shelf below.

6—Keep face to audience; work *with* teachers, not *at* them; observe absolute silence and listening attitude while music is being heard.

7—Make brief statement at beginning of lesson as to purpose of lesson, then let the *real music* do the talking, with only staccato comments on particular applications and uses. Boil your explanations down to the real sugar.

8—Secure attention, interest, response. Work fast, without hurrying; speed up the responses without producing confusion; keep play well in hand.

9—Be dignified but flexible; inspiringly in earnest, yet human.

10—Play only such portion of record as will illustrate the point in hand, except that a masterpiece for cultural hearing should be played entirely. Do not say, "I shall play a *record*," but rather, "Let us listen to_____ (artist) sing (or play)_____(title of composition)." We purvey *music*, not material means.

11—Secure an extra hour of folk dancing out on the lawn after the afternoon session, and make it a prized social feature of the institute.

12—Be prompt; stop on time; subside quickly for next speaker; keep records and material neatly in order, not scattered all over the place.

13—Be an integral part of the institute, not a side-show; listen with interest to the workers in other subjects; fit your remarks and song selections to the spirit of the hour; be on hand throughout the day; stay put, not running away for a siesta as soon as your special hour is over.

MAKE THE MUSIC SERVE

6

LESSON I
INTRODUCTION

DISCUSSION: See "An Appreciation" and "Foreword," *The Victrola in Rural Schools.*

A. Needs.
   1. Necessity of association with good music.
   2. Good music universal heritage of all children, rural and urban.
   3. Material and practical plan for using music in the rural school and community.

B. Aims.
   1. To vitalize the teaching of music.
   2. To give an intelligent and cultural acquaintance with good music.
   3. To form mental habits of
      a. alertness
      b. concentration
      c. imagination
      d. discrimination

C. Plan.
   1. To relate all the music to the life and interests of the child according to modern pedagogy

D. Group singing.
   1. Unifying power of singing together.
   2. Inspirational aid to teachers:

America	17580
Battle Hymn of the Republic	18145
America the Beautiful	18627
Stars of the Summer Night	18627

*E. Appreciation of the beauty and significance of music.

*F. Development of rhythm.

*NOTE: The discussion of points E and F may be postponed until lessons on these subjects are reached.

LESSON II
(Open with Song: **My Old Kentucky Home, 18145**)
RHYTHM: THE FIRST ESSENTIAL

DISCUSSION: Rhythm in life; need in school; value in education and in music study; see *The Victrola in Rural Schools*, page 84, and *Music Appreciation for Little Children*, pages 33–45.

A. Free expression.*

Menuett and Gavotte	17917
March Miniature	64766
Teddy Bears' Picnic	16001

7

The HESITATION

MR. AND MRS. VERNON CASTLE
DANCING THE HESITATION WALTZ

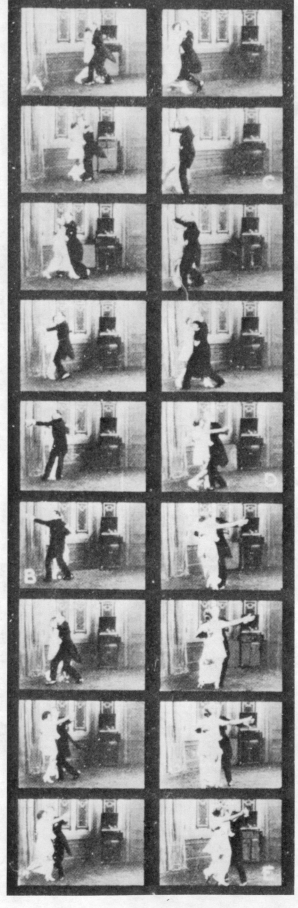

One of several dances illustrated by the popular dancing team of Irene and Vernon Castle in Three Modern Dances. *Camden, New Jersey: Victor Talking Machine Co., 1914. © RCA Records.*

Frances Densmore collected many songs of American Indians for the Smithsonian Institution on cylinder records in the early part of this century.

VICTOR RECORDS OF THE
HESITATION WALTZ

Title	Artist	No.	Size	Price
Girl on the Film—Hesitation Waltzes	Military Band			
Adele Waltzes — Hesitation or Boston	Military Band	35361	12	1.25
Admiration—Waltz Hesitation	Military Band			
Toreador—One-step or Trot	*Military Band*	17524	10	.75
Dreams of Childhood—Waltz Hesitation	Military Band			
Santley Tango (from "When Dreams Come True")	*Military Band*	17466	10	.75
Isle d'amour—Waltz Hesitation	Military Band			
The Flower Garden Ball—Trot	*Military Band*	35346	12	1.25
Espana — Waltz Hesitation	Military Band			
Hydropaten Waltz (with Bells)	*Conway's Band*	35347	12	1.25
Maurice Hesitation Waltz (L'hésitation)	Military Band			
The Poem (La Poéme) (Hesitation or Boston)	Military Band	35355	12	1.25
Miss Caprice—Hesitation or Boston	Military Band			
Marriage Market—Hesitation or Boston	Military Band	35319	12	1.25
Nights of Gladness—Hesitation or Boston	Military Band			
Maori—Tango	*Military Band*	35304	12	1.25
Dreaming — Hesitation or Boston	Military Band			
In the Golden West Medley— One-step	*Military Band*	35295	12	1.25

For other records of the Hesitation—Ask your dealer for complete list of Victor Dance Records

Many small recording companies, along with a special series of Victor and Columbia, were formed to record jazz and country-music performers. From the collection of Carl H. Scheele.

MUSIC   "A Good Man is Hard to Find"—Eddie Green
Bessie Smith, vocal; Porter Grainger, piano; Lincoln
Conway, guitar; 1927; Columbia 1425D.
Reissued: Folkways FJ-2804.

"Fireworks"—Louis Armstrong
Louis Armstrong and His Hot Five: Earl Hines, piano;
Louis Armstrong, trumpet; Fred Robinson, trombone;
Jimmy Strong, clarinet, tenor sax; Mancy Cara, guitar;
Zutty Singleton, drums; 1928; Okeh 8597.
Reissued: Folkways FJ-2809.

"Am I Blue"—Grant Clark, Harry Akst
Ethel Waters, vocal; Tommy Dorsey, trombone; trumpet,
alto sax, clarinet, violin, piano, guitar, bass
unidentified; 1929; Columbia 1837D.
Reissued: Columbia C-3L35.

ACOUSTIC AND ELECTRIC RECORDINGS

At first, all sound recordings were made by the acoustic process. With no amplification, the musicians had to play or sing directly into the recording horn. Electric recording with microphone and amplifier replaced the acoustic process after 1925.

Cornetist recording in La Nature, *August 1889. From Hammer Collection, Smithsonian Institution.*

Some leading recording artists of 1892 included Russell Hunting of the famous "Casey" series, John Y. AtLee, a whistler, and George W. Johnson, a black performer noted for his whistling and laughing records. From The Phonogram, December 1892.

THE PHONOGRAM.

Russell Hunting.
Edw. Issler
Leon Spencer.
Edw. Clarence.
John C. Leach.
George Schweinfest.
John Y. AtLee.
Thomas Bott.
Geo. A. Diamond.
Geo. J. Caskin.
W. F. Denny.
John P. Hogan.
Chas. A. Asbury.
Teddy Simonds.
Geo. W. Johnson.

Young girl recording at a children's party. From Oliver Read Collection.

ACOUSTIC RECORDING

In the acoustic process, the sheer energy from the sounds played or sung into the recording horn caused the diaphragm to vibrate, which in turn caused the stylus to cut into the disc or cylinder. The best early records were of such penetrating sounds as whistlers, military bands, and certain vocal and instrumental soloists.

A singer stood three to four inches from the horn and on high notes moved back, or was pushed back by the recording engineer, to minimize vibrations. For the same reason, a handkerchief was often lowered in

72

Advertisement from The Phonogram, March 1891.

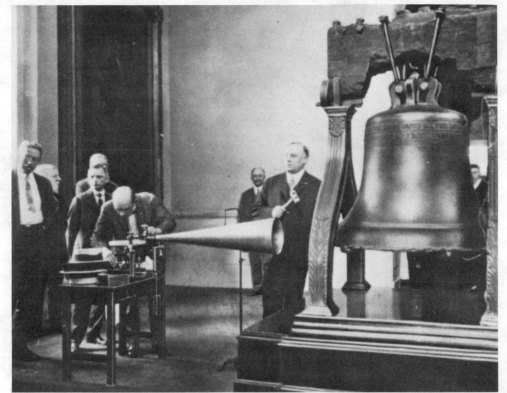

"Stovepipe" at a recording session. From The Talking Machine World, *August 15, 1924.*

Victor Talking Machine Company recording the Liberty Bell. From The Talking Machine World, *July 1917.*

Sousa's Band in a recording session. At least nine recording horns are visible. From The Phonogram, *October 1891.*

front of the horn when a cornet soloist, four to six feet away, hit high notes. For accompaniments, the upright piano was elevated about three feet with its back as close to the horn as possible.

Orchestral groups crowded around the horn, with the louder brass players on bleachers at the rear. Because stringed instruments didn't carry well, scores were often rearranged—bassoons substituting for cellos; tubas for double basses; and Stroh "violins" for the higher strings.

Meeting the growing demand for recordings was a problem. In the early 1890s, it was possible to duplicate cylinder records only by repeating performances. Even with three machines recording at a time, for instance, a singer had to repeat a single selection thirty times to produce even ninety copies. By 1902, however, Edison had begun to mass-produce molded cylinders. Mass production was simpler for disc manufacturers: copies were easily stamped from a matrix made from the wax master.

Enrico Caruso recording for Victor—a self caricature. From RCA Records.

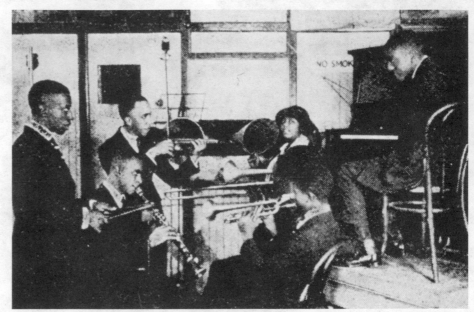

Mamie Smith and Her Jazz Hounds recording "Sax-o-Phoney Blues" at the Okeh Laboratories in New York. From The Talking Machine World, *November 15, 1921.*

Recording session at the Columbia Phonograph Co. From The Phonoscope, *July 1898.*

William Jennings Bryan recording for Gennett Records. From The Talking Machine World, *August 15, 1923.*

Early 20th-century recording scene. From RCA Records.

Edison music room in 1903. From Edison National Monument.

Making violin-solo records at the Edison studio. Cover of Scientific
American, *December 22, 1900.*

Making band records at the Edison studio. Cover of Scientific American, *December 22, 1900.*

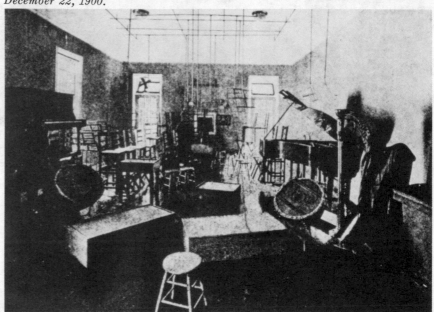

Recording studio. From Scientific American, *August 31, 1918. Reprinted with permission.*

Jacques Urlus with Cesare Sodero, conductor, recording at the Edison studio March 30, 1916. From Edison National Monument.

"Playing for a record—Not to Break One, but to Make One. These players are so grouped that the horn at the rear will catch the tones of all the instruments in a proper blend without the over—or under—emphasis of any one of them. Courtesy of the Graphophone Company." From The Literary Digest, September 28, 1918.

A Gennett recording session in 1924 with Bix and his Rhythm Jugglers. From right to left are Tommy Dorsey, Bix Beiderbecke, Don Murray, Paul Mertz, Tommy Gorgano, and Howdy Quicksell. From Leo Walker Collection.

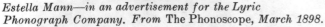

Estella Mann—in an advertisement for the Lyric Phonograph Company. From The Phonoscope, March 1898.

Charlie Chaplin directing the recording of his compositions with Abe Lyman and his California Orchestra. From The Talking Machine World, August 15, 1925.

Casting and turning blank records at the Edison factory. Cover of Scientific American, December 22, 1900.

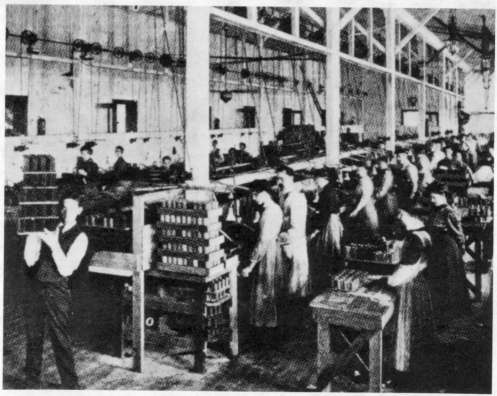

Testing the phonographs at Edison. Cover of Scientific American, *December 22, 1900.*

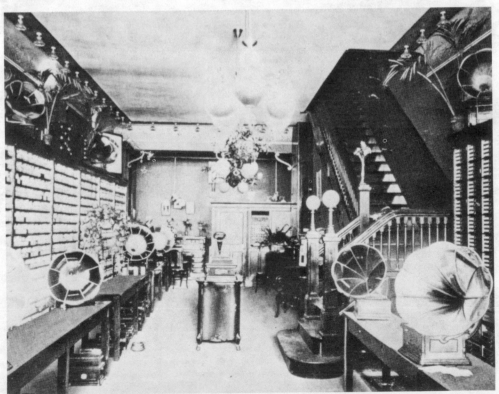

Once the records were made, they could be purchased in stores similar to this one of 1907. From archive of Frederick Fried, New York.

STROH VIOLIN

A major shortcoming of acoustic recording was the lack of carrying power of string instruments. To overcome this, Charles Stroh introduced a new "violin" in England in 1901. He replaced the usual wooden body with a metal resonator to produce a louder, more penetrating sound. The horn at the end of the fingerboard directed this sound either into the recording horn or into the ear of the singer. The performer placed the small horn attached to the resonator at his ear in order to hear what he was playing more distinctly.

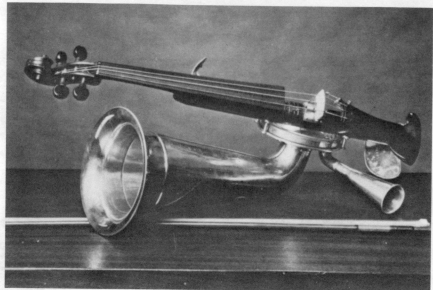

Stroh violin, early 20th century. Lent by Arne B. Larson Collection. (Lautman photo 77198.)

Rosario Bourdon conducting the Victor Salon Orchestra in an acoustic-recording session at Victor. Note the man in right foreground playing the Stroh violin. From Clark Collection, Smithsonian Institution.

ELECTRIC RECORDING

In 1925 phonograph recording changed drastically: a microphone replaced the recording horn. The energy of the sounds of the recording musicians was converted in the microphone to electric currents, which were amplified to drive a cutting stylus.

With the use of microphone and amplifier, it was possible for musicians to record under conditions closer to a concert-hall experience. The result was a greatly improved sound and often a more spontaneous performance. Nuance of dynamics was at last possible. Because strings now recorded better, orchestras could play works as written rather than with arrangements to compensate for variations in recording power.

Much refined since its early days when the sibilants hissed and the bass boomed, electric recording—whether on tape or disc— is still the process used by phonograph companies today.

This electric-recording session involves the same musicians as in the photograph at left; but with the use of a microphone, the seating arrangement is similar to a concert performance. From RCA Records.

AUTOMATIC ORTHOPHONIC VICTROLA

The Orthophonic talking machine symbolizes the end of acoustic recording. Fitted with a new reproducer and an enclosed exponential horn especially designed for electric recordings, the Orthophonic also had an automatic record changer, a mechanism for record buyers interested in full-length orchestral and operatic works.

The console model also symbolizes the phonograph's evolution from a machine in the corner of the parlor to an elaborate and expensive piece of furniture that held a place of honor in living rooms.

Automatic Orthophonic Victrola, 1927. Made by Victor Talking Machine Co., Camden, New Jersey. Gift of Oliver Read. Catalog number 324,198. (Lautman photo 77371.)

The Orthophonic when not in use. Catalog number 324,198. (Lautman photo 77372.)

To change a selection, a metal ring lifted the record off the turntable. A release mechanism then sent the record sliding down a chute to a padded drawer below. Catalog number 324,198. (Lautman photo 77373.)

MUSIC   "Yes! We Have No Bananas"—Frank Silver, Irving Cohn
Irving Kaufman, vocal; Selvin's Orchestra; 1921.
Vocalion (The Aeolian Co.) A-14590.

"When the Moon Comes over the Mountain"—Kate Smith
and Howard Johnson, Harry Woods
Kate Smith, vocal; Jack Miller and His Orchestra; 1931;
Clarion 5359.
Reissued: Harmony HS-11353.

"My Time is Your Time"—Eric Little, Leo Dance
Rudy Vallée and His Connecticut Yankees, 1942.
Reissued: RCA Victor, LPM-2507.

"Keep on the Sunny Side"—A.P. Carter
The Carter Family; 1935; Bluebird 33-0537.
Reissued: Harmony HS-11332.

"Where the Blue of the Night Meets the Gold of the Day"—
Roy Turk, Bing Crosby, Fred E. Ahlert
Bing Crosby, vocal; 1931; Brunswick 6226.

"The Man I Love"—Ira and George Gershwin
Vaughn De Leath, vocal; Paul Whiteman and His Orchestra:
Bix Beiderbecke, cornet; Charlie Margulis, Harry Goldfield,
Ed Pinder, trumpets; Boyce Cullen, Wilbur Hall, Bill Rank,
Jack Fulton, trombones; Irving Friedman, clarinet; Irving
Friedman, Chester Hazlett, alto saxes; Frankie Trumbauer,
C-melody sax; Rube Crozier, Roy Maier, tenor saxes;
Charles Strickfadden, baritone sax; Kurt Dieterle,
Mischa Russell, Charles Gaylord, violins; Matty Malneck,
viola; Roy Bargy, Lennie Hayton, pianos; Mike Pingatore,
banjo; Mike Trafficante, bass; Min Leibrook, tuba;
George Marsh, drums; Ferde Grofé, arranger; 1928;
Columbia 50068D.

Reissued: Columbia C-3L35.

THE IMPACT OF RADIO

Radio created a national audience that could
listen simultaneously for the first time to a
steady flow of free entertainment. Improved
microphone and related audio equipment
resulted in a new, intimate, and relaxed style
of performance.

Bing Crosby during a broadcast in 1935. From CBS.

During the 1920s radio caught the fancy of Americans everywhere, and by the 1930s it had become almost a necessity of life to ease the hardships of the Depression.

Music dominated the programming of the early days of radio: music from live performers (at first unpaid), phonographs, and player pianos. Later, programming became more diversified with news and sports broadcasts, drama, variety shows, soap operas, and star comedians and musicians.

When the majority of the variety programs were transferred to television in the late 1940s, radio schedules once again listed mostly music—recordings selected by disc jockeys.

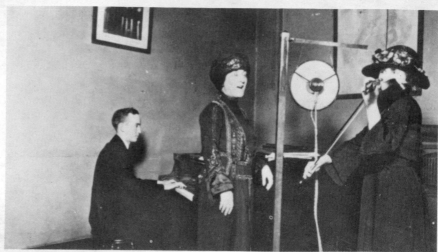

Live music from a broadcast studio of 1922. From District of Columbia Public Library.

Vladimir Rosery, a Russian tenor, singing "Lord Randall" at WJZ, Newark, February 6, 1922. Note the phonograph at right. From Westinghouse.

Eddie Cantor broadcasting from KDKA in Pittsburgh about 1923. From Clark Collection. Smithsonian Institution.

Members of the Carter Family, well-known country music performers, have entertained thousands of radio listeners. "Mother Maybelle" (left) still performs with her daughters and, on occasion, with her son-in-law, Johnny Cash. From collection of Ralph Rinzler.

Opera stars such as Lily Pons were heard not only on broadcasts of full-length operas, but also on variety shows like the André Kostelanetz Chesterfield Hour, about 1940. © M. Robert Rogers.

86

"Uncle Dave" Macon (right) and his son, Dorris, performing for the "Grand Ole Opry" on WSM, Nashville. The Opry was and is a Saturday night institution for millions of listeners. From collection of Ralph Rinzler.

The NBC Symphony Orchestra under the direction of Arturo Toscanini was one of several programs that brought classical music into the homes of listeners far removed from metropolitan centers. From NBC.

Major Bowes, whose talent show was one of the most popular radio programs in the mid-1930s, is shown here with the Hoboken Four in 1935. At far right is Frank Sinatra. From collection of Lewis Graham.

Arthur Godfrey in his early disc-jockey days in Washington, D.C. From CBS.

The Kate Smith Hour in the 1930s. From District of Columbia Public Library.

THE MICROPHONE

The microphone symbolized the link between the radio performer and his unseen audience. Broadcasting from an isolated studio, the performer's music and comments were amplified and transmitted to homes and automobiles throughout the country.

One of the most popular of this new breed of radio entertainer was the crooner, whose singing style depended heavily upon electronic amplification equipment.

Radio broadcast being heard through the horn on the shelf in this kitchen of the mid-1920s. From Clark Collection, Smithsonian Institution.

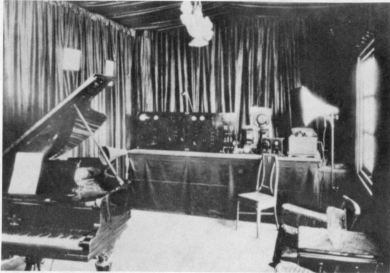

This interior of the Westinghouse station in San Francisco in 1927 shows how isolated a performer could be from his listeners. From Clark Collection, Smithsonian Institution.

Listening to the radio on an outing in the country. From The Talking Machine World, *May 1928.*

By the 1930s the isolated room was often replaced by large studio theaters filled with an audience. This picture shows Freddy Martin and his Orchestra in the early 1940s. From collection of Leo Walker.

Vaughn De Leath, "The Original Radio Girl," and sometimes called the first crooner, broadcasting from WJZ, Newark, New Jersey, in 1921. From Clark Collection, Smithsonian Institution.

Learn to Croon

SUNG BY
BING CROSBY
IN THE PARAMOUNT PICTURE
"COLLEGE HUMOR"

LYRIC BY
SAM COSLOW
MUSIC BY
ARTHUR JOHNSTON

Famous Music

This type of singing became so popular that Bing Crosby, a crooner par excellence, sang a song about it in a movie in 1933. By Permission of Famous Music Corp.

Another crooner, whose singing aroused the adulation of thousands of loyal (often swooning) fans, was Frank Sinatra, seen here singing on "Your Hit Parade" in the 1940s. From CBS.

Rudy Vallée, a popular radio singer of the 1930s, who also conducted an orchestra, crooned not only through a microphone but also through a megaphone. From NBC.

Carbon microphone from WFLA, Tampa, Florida. Made about 1923 by Western Electric Co. Gift of National Broadcasting Co. Catalog number 311,445. (77136B.) The shape of the microphone changed through the years, sometimes because of technical improvements, sometimes to camouflage it for a performer frozen with "mike fright."

Wooden-horn microphone used by Metropolitan Opera star Ann Case, who sang "Ave Maria" in one of the first remote broadcasts from an improvised studio at the New York Electrical Show in October 1921. From RCA.

"Soup plate" microphone used by Lydia Lipkooska, coloratura soprano, at WJZ, Newark, New Jersey, in 1922. Westinghouse photo.

Carbon microphone used by Dr. Sigmund Spaeth, educator, lecturer, and journalist, who gave popular talks on music appreciation. He is shown here at WDR, New York, in the 1920s.

"Tomato can" microphone at KDKA, Pittsburgh, in the 1920s. From Westinghouse.

Microphone camouflaged as a globe in the 1920s. From Clark Collection, Smithsonian Institution.

Condenser microphone used by Ethel Waters on NBC in 1933. From NBC.

Ribbon microphone used by Margaret Whiting, Jack Smith, and Dinah Shore on the CBS Jack Smith Show in 1949. From CBS.

Dynamic microphone used by Billie Holliday.

WHAT ARE THE WILD WIRES SAYING?

Drawing by Charles Dana Gibson from Life, 1922.

RADIO RECEIVING SETS

The excitement shared by those who listened to early radio broadcasts spread to their neighbors and friends. Since most manufacturers were unprepared for this sudden popularity, many home receivers in the early 1920s were put together from parts purchased at radio supply stores or from plans supplied by the National Bureau of Standards.

People on the East Coast would stay up all night to hear a voice that arrived miraculously through the air from Pittsburgh or Chicago. Despite crackling noise or fading sound, radio seemed to offer great promise to America and to the world. Reflecting this optimism, Herbert Hoover, then Secretary of Commerce and in charge of regulating radio, stated in the early 1920s that it was "inconceivable that we should allow so great a possibility for service to be drowned in advertising chatter."

Everyone was listening to the radio in the 1920s. From Library of Congress.

CRYSTAL SETS, HEADPHONES, AND CRYSTAL RECEIVERS

The earliest home broadcasts were heard through headphone-and-crystal sets. Some receivers allowed more than one set of headphones to be attached at one time.

This simple crystal set was made about 1921 by the National Bureau of Standards, but could be constructed at home from spare pieces of wood, wires, and an old Quaker Oats box. Instructions were printed by the Bureau of Standards. Catalog number 313,513. (Lautman photo 77359.)

Men in a hospital listening to a radio in the early 1920s. From Westinghouse.

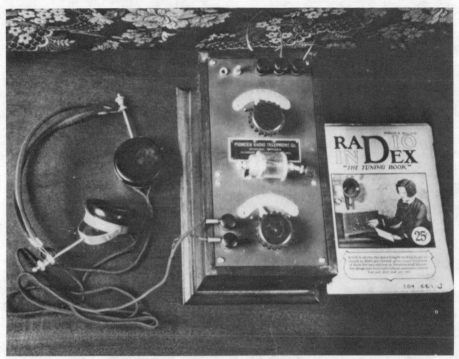

Murdock headphone, about 1924.
Crystal set, about 1924, custom-made by Pioneer Radio Telephone Co., New York.
Gift of Mrs. Susan Horle. Catalog number 314,116. (Lautman photo 77354.)

Listeners enjoying a crystal set in the early 1920s. From KDKA.

LOUDSPEAKERS AND BROADCAST RECEIVERS

The crystal set was replaced by a more sophisticated receiver equipped with the triode, the three-electron vacuum tube developed by Lee De Forest that made it possible to amplify the radio signal.

De Forest receiver, 1925, made by De Forest Radio Co., Jersey City, New Jersey. Gift of Dr. Lee De Forest. Catalog number 313,640. Western Electric loudspeaker, made about 1923 by Western Electric Co. Gift of Miss E. P. Custiss. Catalog number 314,693. (Lautman photos 77355, 77191.)

Lee De Forest is shown holding an early version of the triode. Because the triode helped to amplify sounds, it became an important element in the change to electric recording by 1925. De Forest also developed a process of sound-on-film.

Detail of De Forest receiver showing electron tubes. Catalog number 314,693. (Lautman photo 77356.)

Radiola loudspeaker, made about 1928 by RCA. Catalog number 317,874. (Lautman photo 77194.)

Enjoying radio music on a picnic. From The Talking Machine World. *April 15, 1925.*

A young man learns to play the harmonica on the Hohner Harmonica Hour weekly over WEAF, New York. From The Talking Machine World, *February 15, 1925.*

Atwater Kent floor model. 1930 model 70 receiver made by Atwater Kent Mfg. Co., Philadelphia. Catalog number 321,426. (Lautman photo 77377.)

FLOOR MODEL

The radio evolved from a collection of machinery into a piece of furniture, as the phonograph had earlier. Floor-model radios were found in many homes after 1930.

97

I. MUSICALS OF THE THIRTIES

1. *Forty-Second Street*, Warner Brothers, 1933.
   Song—"Shuffle Off to Buffalo"—Harry Akst
   and Ruby Keeler (Ginger Rogers in chorus).
   Directed by Lloyd Bacon.

2. *Gold Diggers of Broadway*, First National Pictures, 1935.
   Song—"The Words Are In My Heart"—Dick Powell.
   Directed by Busby Berkeley.

3. *Flying Down to Rio*, RKO, 1933.
   Song—"Carioca"—Fred Astaire and Ginger Rogers.
   Directed by Thornton Freeland.

II. HIGHLIGHTS OF M-G-M MUSICALS:
1930s—1950s. Produced by Arthur Freed.

1. *The Songwriters* (M-G-M short), 1929.
   Song—"Wedding of the Painted Doll"—Arthur Freed;
   introduced by Jack Benny.
   Directed by Charles Reisner.

2. *Babes in Arms*, 1939.
   Title Song—Judy Garland and Mickey Rooney.
   Directed by Busby Berkeley.

3. *For Me and My Gal*, 1942.
   Title Song—Judy Garland and Gene Kelly.
   Directed by Busby Berkeley.

4. *Meet Me in St. Louis*, 1944.
   "The Trolley Song"—Judy Garland.
   Directed by Vincente Minnelli.

5. *Ziegfeld Follies*, 1946.
   "The Babbitt and the Bromide"—Gene Kelly and Fred Astaire.
   Directed by Vincente Minnelli.

6. *On the Town*, 1949.
   Song—"New York, New York."—Gene Kelly, Frank Sinatra,
   and Jules Munshin.
   Directed by Gene Kelly and Stanley Donen.

7. *Easter Parade*, 1948.
   Title Song—Judy Garland and Fred Astaire.
   Directed by Charles Walters.

8. *Annie Get Your Gun*, 1950.
   "There's No Business Like Show Business" by Betty Hutton,
   Howard Keel, Keenan Wynn, and Louis Calhern.
   Directed by George Sidney.

9. *Showboat*, 1957.
   "Can't Help Lovin' That Man"—Ava Gardner.
   "Ol' Man River"—William Warfield.
   Directed by George Sidney.

10. *American in Paris*, 1957.
    Concerto in F by George Gershwin—Oscar Levant.
    Portion of ballet *American in Paris*—Gene Kelly and
    Leslie Caron.
    Directed by Vincente Minnelli.

11. *Singin' in the Rain*, 1952.
    Title Song—Gene Kelly.
    Directed by Gene Kelly and Stanley Donen.

MOVIES AND MUSIC

By the early 1930s movies began to provide
"100% All Talking*All Singing*All Dancing!"
entertainment. The best of movie musicals and
animated cartoons imaginatively combined
image and music.

Fred Astaire and Ginger Rogers in
The Barkleys of Broadway, *1949. From MGM.*

DEPARTMENT OF SPECIAL Public Entertainment Outfits and Supplies

It has bee
lic entertain
field and an
with a very
that there h
energy expe
lack of kno
complete a s
ment, and mo
work success
inently in sigh
and are glad to
we have made
work so simple

Not only ha
up Complete En
advertising matte
thing necessary to
money making
each outfit a bo
the plainest an
the outfits, he
use of halls, c
thing that i
know or that

THIS SP
is in charge
communicat'
country, an
very plain a
book, he wil
who has purc
ing any questi
the purchase of
you would like
as we may be th
cessful, strictly
ing business.

THE QU
this departm
absolutely nec
undone that
our patrons, f
on theirs.

WE FULLY GUARANTEE the quality of everything we sell in this line and if on receipt of the goods they are not found to be exactly as represented, they can be returned to us and all money paid will be cheerfully refunded. **OUR PRICES ARE THE LOWEST** at which first-class goods in this line have ever been sold. In fact, some of our outfits are sold at about one-half of the prices at which similar goods are sold by some of the oldest houses in this line of business. Dealers in this class of goods have been educated to very large profits and on that basis they are content with a small number of sales, but with small sales they must buy in small quantities for which reason they pay for some of their goods nearly twice what we do. **WE CONTRACT FOR LARGE QUANTITIES** of these goods and are thus enabled to purchase at the lowest prices and as we are satisfied with the smallest possible margin for profit, it can be plainly seen why we can undersell other dealers. A comparison of our goods and prices with those of other houses will demonstrate to those who are familiar with the goods what a great amount of money we can save for them, but we want it borne in mind at all times that we are in etitio ly with first-class goods. Goods of inferior quality in this price; in fact, they are practically orthless, as they will ment and di a exhibit

OUR VERY LIBERAL TER
D., subject to a thorough examination the required deposit is sent with order quired on orders up to $15.00. $2.00 on amination, the goods are not found to returned to us and the money dep

ADVANTAGES OF SENDING accompanies the order the customer charges for collection and return packing and examining the outfit station is avoided. The outfit can everything is not found to be exactly ing opportunity they can be ret cheerfully refunded.

An advertisement from the Sears catalog of 1898 shows a lantern-slide outfit. The man on the stage seems to be ready to operate the phonograph beside him. From Warshaw Collection of Business Americana, Smithsonian Institution.

Even in the late 19th century, music and picture machines were combined to provide entertainment. People flocked to theaters to see lantern slides, accompanied by lectures and recorded songs. Amusement-arcade operators usually offered both kinetoscopes and talking machines. In the early 20th century, lantern slides or stereoscopic pictures were synchronized with cylinder records in one machine—Rosenfield's Illustrated Song Machine.

As moviemakers began to produce longer works, music played a vital part in creating a dramatic atmosphere in an otherwise silent production. In large urban theaters, a full orchestra provided music cued to reel and scene. Most smaller theaters had either a pianist or organist, or a mechanical paper-roll instrument to create the impression of a pit orchestra.

Early attempts to synchronize recorded sound and moving pictures were unsuccessful because of the unreliability of the pulley systems that stretched the length of the theaters to link the projectors and the talking machines. By the 1920s studios began to introduce movies synchronized more successfully with Vitaphone records, usually playing background music only.

100

An early Edison film strip showing an acoustic-recording scene. From Edison National Monument.

Prelude.

Pages from the musical score composed by William Furst
for the silent movie Joan the Woman, starring Metropolitan
Opera soprano Geraldine Farrar and produced by
Cecil B. De Mille in 1917. From E. C. Schirmer.

Instructions to the conductor.

A dramatic moment near the end.

The interior of a 1922 Fotoplayer Style 25.
From Vestal Press Collection.

The left section of the instrument: chest holds
bass pipes, train whistle, thunder, bass drum,
tom-tom, cymbal, sleigh bells, and glockenspiel;

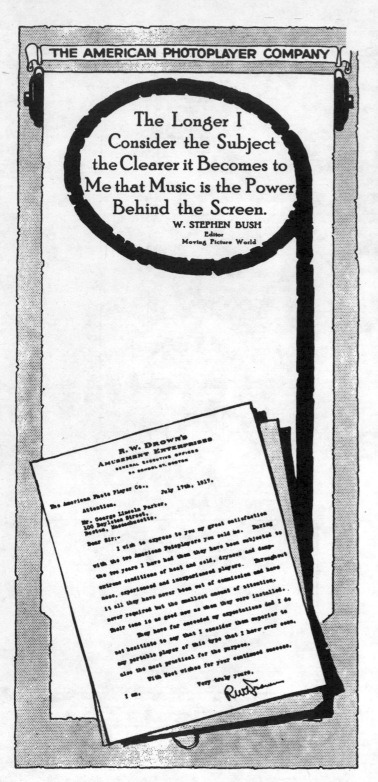

THE AMERICAN PHOTOPLAYER COMPANY

The Longer I
Consider the Subject
the Clearer it Becomes to
Me that Music is the Power
Behind the Screen.

W. STEPHEN BUSH
Editor
Moving Picture World

Pages from a "Fotoplayer" brochure of 1918.
Note the many effects possible on this machine.
From Vestal Press Collection.

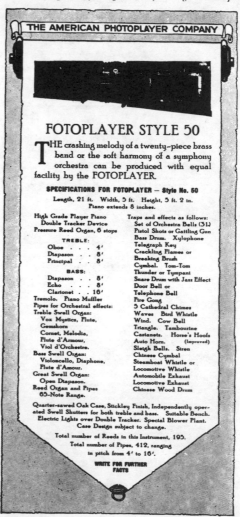

THE AMERICAN PHOTOPLAYER COMPANY

FOTOPLAYER STYLE 50

THE crashing melody of a twenty-piece brass
band or the soft harmony of a symphony
orchestra can be produced with equal
facility by the FOTOPLAYER.

SPECIFICATIONS FOR FOTOPLAYER — Style No. 50

Length, 21 ft. Width, 5 ft. Height, 5 ft. 2 in.
Piano extends 8 inches.

High Grade Player Piano
Double Tracker Device
Pressure Reed Organ, 6 stops

TREBLE:

Oboe	. . .	4'
Diapason	. .	8'
Principal	. .	8'

BASS:

Diapason	. .	8'
Echo	. . .	8'
Clarionet	. .	16'

Tremolo. Piano Muffler
Pipes for Orchestral effects:
Treble Swell Organ:
Vox Mystics, Flute,
Gemshorn
Cornet, Melodia,
Flute d'Amour,
Viol d'Orchestre.
Bass Swell Organ:
Violoncello, Diaphone,
Flute d'Amour.
Great Swell Organ:
Open Diapason.
Reed Organ and Pipes
65-Note Range.

Traps and effects as follows:
Set of Orchestra Bells (31)
Pistol Shots or Gatling Gun
Bass Drum. Xylophone
Telegraph Key
Crackling Flames or
Breaking Brush
Cymbal. Tom-Tom
Thunder or Tympant
Snare Drum with Jazz Effect
Door Bell or
Telephone Bell
Fire Gong
5 Cathedral Chimes
Waves Bird Whistle
Wind. Cow Bell
Triangle. Tambourine
Castanets. Horse's Hoofs
Auto Horn.   (Improved)
Sleigh Bells. Siren
Chinese Cymbal
Steamboat Whistle or
Locomotive Whistle
Automobile Exhaust
Locomotive Exhaust
Chinese Wood Drum

Quarter-sawed Oak Case, Stickley Finish, Independently oper-
ated Swell Shutters for both treble and bass. Suitable Bench.
Electric Lights over Double Tracker. Special Blower Plant.
Case Design subject to change.

Total number of Reeds in this Instrument, 195.

Total number of Pipes, 412, ranging
in pitch from 4' to 16'.

WRITE FOR FURTHER
FACTS

The center section: Kohler and Campbell piano has a duplex music-roll arrangement that permits quick switches between two types of mood music;

And at right: chest contains klaxon, castanet, tambourine, Chinese crash cymbal, wind, pistol shot, cathedral gong, and two ranks of pipes.

No.	Title	Composer	Price
9	Agitato No. 9	Adapted from Grieg	.85

Great for fights, quarrels, approaching disaster, fear. Classified as—
    Agitato—Fight.
    Agitato—Light.
    Hurry—Dramatic.
    Tension—Dramatic.

12 Sorrow, Sadness, Desolation.................. E. B. Sawtelle .85

This will bring the tears with scenes of deep pathos. Classified as—
    Dramatic—Light.
    Pathetic—Low.
    Pathetic—Strong.

13 A Little Sob Music..........Dixie Johnson .75

Another strong number for sob scenes. Classified as—
    Charactertistic—Church (Played Slow)
    Pathetic—Light.
    Sentimental—Plaintive.

***14 Love Scene Music**..........E. E. McCargar .75

An appealing melody, slightly pathetic. Classified as—
    Love Theme—Quiet (PP—Slow).
    Love Theme—Strong.
    Pathetic—Narrative.
    Sentimental—Light.

15 Sob Sister....................E. B. Sawtelle .90

A quiet love theme, strongly sentimental. Classified as—
    Love Theme—Quiet.
    Pathetic—Slow.
    Pathetic—Sweet.
    Sentimental—Strong.

16 "Reuben and Rachel"....................Gooch .75

Country—Jay music, pure and simple. Classified as—
    Comedy—Rube.

17 Mushy Music........................Jack Russell .85

Adds fifty per cent to tender-moment scenes. Classified as—
    Love Theme—Quiet.
    Pathetic—High.
    Pathetic—Light.
    Sentimental—Strong.

***18 Molly Darling**................................Hays .80

An appealing, old-fashioned love theme. Classified as—
    Love Theme—Old Fashioned.
    Sentimental—Light.

19 Battle Hymn of the Republic........Steffe .85

An exceptional arrangement of "John Brown's Body." Classified as—
    Patriotic.

* Organ arrangement—not suitable for player piano.
ADD 5% WAR TAX

Six

No.	Title	Composer	Price
20	Elegie, Melodie	Massenet	.90

For bereavement, hopelessness, desolation, what is more fitting than this masterpiece? Wonderful organ solo effects—Classified as—
    Pathetic—Deep.
    Pathetic—Slow.

***21 Norway Waltz**....................Eddie Horton .75

Exceptionally fine waltz for use on organs. Classified as—
    Neutral—Waltz.

22 War—Battle Music....................Adapted from Beethoven .80

All that the name implies. Classified as—
    Agitato—Battle.
    Agitato—Storm.

23 Hurry! Hurry! No. 7..............Adapted from Rubinstein .90

This will make fires, riots, strikes, mobs, etc., register 100%. Classified as—
    Agitato—Light.
    Hurry—Dramatic.

25 I Am a Bold Policeman........Jack Russell .75

Great for sneaky stuff in comedy. Classified as—
    Comedy—Sneaky.
    Mysterious—Comic.

26 Action Furioso................Eddie Horton .75

Thrill stuff from start to finish. Classified as—
    Agitato—Fight.
    Agitato—Low.
    Tension—Dramatic.

27 Drunk, Soused, Spree........................ .85

This never fails to bring a laugh when played with "Jag" action. Classified as—
    Comedy—Jag.

28 Agitato No. 11........Adapted from Liszt .90

Another one—all thrills. Classified as—
    Agitato—Joyful.
    Hurry—Merry.

29 Sentiment—A Reverie......E. B. Sawtelle .90

A plaintive, old-fashioned love theme. Classified as—
    Love Theme—Old Fashioned.
    Pathetic—Light.
    Sentimental—Plaintive.
    Sentimental—Strong.

* Organ arrangement—not suitable for player piano.
ADD 5% WAR TAX
Seven

A sample page from the Complete Catalogue of Picturolls, Sherman Clay & Co., November 1918. From Vestal Press Collection.

Al Jolson singing in a California cabaret in
The Jazz Singer, 1927. From Museum of
Modern Art.

With great fanfare, Warner Brothers presented
Al Jolson in "The Jazz Singer" to the public in 1927.
Although still mainly using subtitles and hearts-and-
flowers orchestral themes, the movie included a few
scenes in which Jolson actually talked and sang.

   After that success, moviemakers became obsessed with
sound. In the 1930s all-talking, all-singing, all-dancing
movies dominated the industry. And the animated
cartoons of Walt Disney introduced an ingenious new
combination of sound and image.

   Sound-on-film, developed independently by Lee De
Forest in America and, among others, Tri-Ergon in
Germany, became standard after 1931. This method of
recording the sound directly on one edge of the film
strip by a photoelectric process solved the problem of
synchronization.

   Since the 1930s music has been used not only for
musicals but also to set moods, create suspense, and
produce other effects not possible with the musical
104 accompaniment of an earlier time.

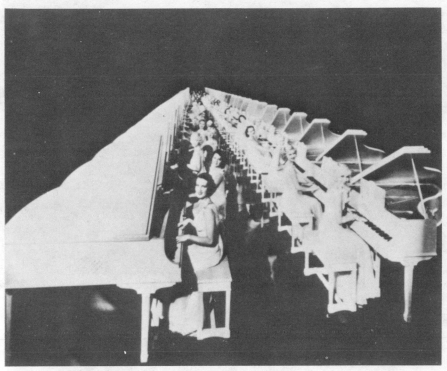

Scene from The Gold Diggers of Broadway (1935), *famous for the elaborate choreography by Busby Berkeley. From Museum of Modern Art.*

Gene Kelly, as did Fred Astaire in other movies, creatively combines song and dance in this scene from Singin' in the Rain. *From MGM.*

The three pigs sing "Who's Afraid of the Big Bad Wolf?" in Walt Disney's Three Little Pigs *of 1933. The song gave spirit to many during the Depression years. From Walt Disney Productions.*

MUSIC   "O Lady Be Good"—Ira and George Gershwin
Ella Fitzgerald, vocal; Bob Haggart and His Orchestra:
Chris Griffin, Andy Ferretti, Bob Peck, trumpets;
Will Bradley, Jack Satterfield, Fred Orms, trombones;
Ernie Caceres, baritone sax; Stan Freeman, piano;
Danny Perri, guitar; Bob Haggart, Mory Feld, basses;
1947; Decca 23956.
Reissued: Decca DL-79245.

"Begin the Beguine"—Cole Porter
Artie Shaw and His Orchestra, 1938; Bluebird B-7746B
Reissued: RCA Victor 27546B

"I'll Never Smile Again"—Ruth Lowe
Frank Sinatra, vocal; Tommy Dorsey and His Orchestra, 1940;
Victor 26628.
Reissued: RCA Victor 27521A.

THE JUKEBOX CRAZE

The jukebox in the 1930s and early 1940s was as important in molding America's taste in popular music as was the disc jockey after World War II. It brought performers fame through constant exposure and helped to revive the phonograph by creating a national market for popular records.

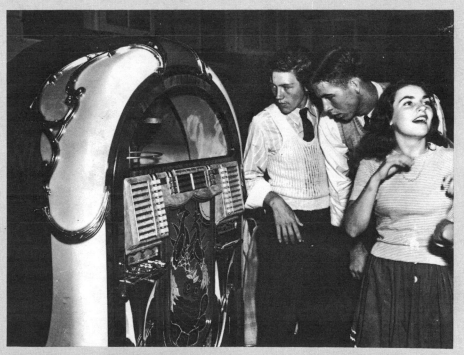

Teenagers in Richwood, West Virginia, listening to music from a Wurlitzer jukebox in the early 1940s. Farm Security Administration photo by John Collin, September 1942. From Library of Congress.

The jukebox was everywhere—in restaurants, resort hotels, wartime canteens, honky tonks, school auditoriums, ice-cream parlors, and taverns that opened after the repeal of Prohibition. While the South and Southwest favored country music, and black communities preferred gospel songs and blues, most of the country spent nickels on swing and the latest Broadway hits.

The Seeburg Company dubbed this their Minute Man model to promote the sale of defense bonds during World War II. From Seeburg Corp.

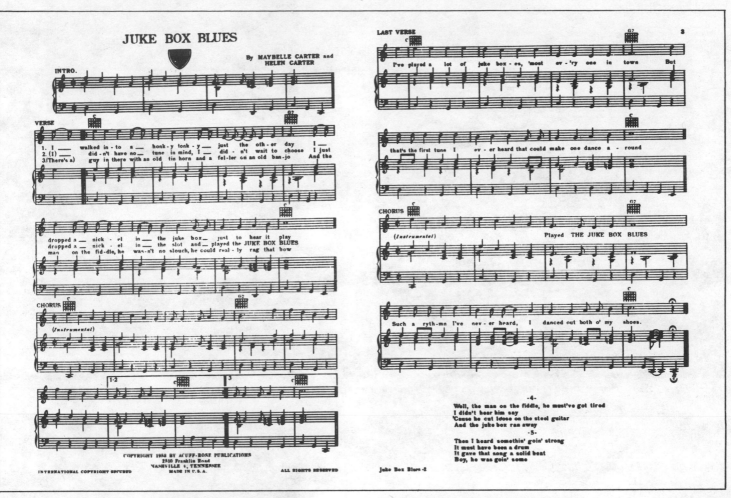

Couple dancing to Seeburg jukebox in the mid-1940s. From Seeburg Corp.

A few of the star musicians often heard on the jukebox.

Peggy Lee (resting on an early 1950s jukebox equipped with 45-rpm records).

Louis Armstrong.

Duke Ellington.

Gene Autry in 1952. From CBS.

Benny Goodman in 1937. From collection of D. Russell Connor.

Elvis Presley in the 1950s. From RCA.

Harry James in 1944. From collection of Leo Walker.

WURLITZER JUKEBOX

The jukebox exterior, as well as its mechanism, was in a class by itself. The Wurlitzer Company provided especially imaginative cases for its models—from peacocks to bubbling kinetic sculpture.

HIT TUNES	TOP FORTY	GOLDEN OLDIES	RHYTHM & BLUES	CLASSICAL	HOT COUNTRY	POLKAS	NOVELTY	WALTZES

List of tune categories provided for jukebox operators in 1970. From Wurlitzer Co.

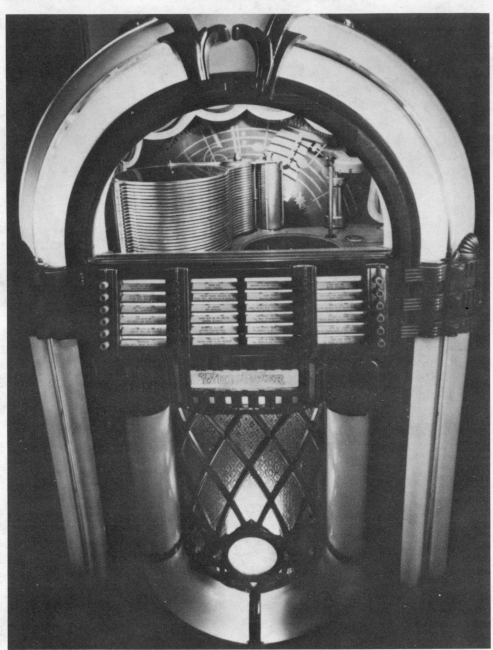

View of Wurlitzer Model 1015, the bubbler, 1946. Made by Wurlitzer Co., North Tonawanda, New York.
Gift of Roth Novelty Co. Catalog number 71.11 (Lautman photo 77370.)

Rockola Multi-Selector of 1935, one of the more subdued models. From Rockola Manufacturing Corp.

MUSIC   "Menuetto" from Symphony in C, Opus 21—Ludwig
van Beethoven, NBC Symphony Orchestra, Arturo
Toscanini, conductor, 1951.
RCA Victor LM-6901.

"Ready Teddy"—Blackwell Marascalco
Elvis Presley, vocal and guitar, 1956.
RCA Victor LPM-1382.

"Blowin' in the Wind"—Bob Dylan
Bob Dylan, vocal and guitar, 1960.
Columbia CL-1986.

SEMPER FIDELITY

For decades the discerning listener—known in audio circles as the "golden ear"—had been demanding improved home reproduction of music. **A** new era in listening was created in the 1950s when manufacturers began mass-producing high-fidelity audio equipment, **FM** radios, tape machines, and long-playing records.

William Steig drawing on the cover of the Columbia recording, "Delirium in Hi-Fi." From Columbia Records.

A series of photographs of Arturo Toscanini recording Schubert's C Major Symphony on 78s with the Philadelphia Orchestra at the Academy of Music on December 14, 1941. © M. Robert Rogers.

Toscanini, guest conductor, confers with Eugene Ormandy, conductor of the Philadelphia Orchestra, before the recording begins.

The orchestra listens to Toscanini while Charles O'Connell, music director for Victor Red Seal Records, stands by. The recording was made with a single microphone pick-up.

Toscanini, O'Connell (right), and the orchestra listen (top photo) to playback. At center, Toscanini points out a mistake as O'Connell reacts to the idea of re-recording. Below, the cello section (lower left) is not happy with this section of the playback.

In the control room, the master disc is cut on the spot. Engineers man the simple controls and O'Connell (seated) follows the score.

Before any record was released, Toscanini had to approve the proof pressing at RCA Victor in Camden, New Jersey. With his wife he is shown listening to the music through triple coaxial speakers in early 1942.

117

In 1961 Dr. Peter Goldmark, president and director of Research at CBS Laboratories, presented to the Smithsonian Institution this successful experimental long-playing record developed by him and his associates in 1945. Catalog number 319,554. (77123)

REVOLUTIONS IN RECORD MAKING

As World War II ended, record manufacturers were producing shellac discs which, when rotated at 78 revolutions per minute (rpm), played about four minutes of music.

In 1948 Columbia Records introduced the revolutionary long-playing record (LP), a twelve-inch unbreakable disc cut with micro-grooves and designed to revolve at 33⅓ rpm. Columbia also introduced a necessary element

Edward Wallerstein, board chairman of Columbia Records; Goddard Lieberson, then vice-president of Columbia Masterworks; and conductor Fritz Reiner listen to an LP record on a low-priced player developed by Philco in 1948. From Columbia Records.

Dr. Peter Goldmark, standing beside a pile of 78 records, holds a corresponding amount of music on LP records. From CBS Laboratories.

The RCA Victor 45-rpm record player could be attached to any radio. From RCA.

The 45-rpm player was also found in the DuMont Bradford television set of 1949. From Dumont Collection, Smithsonian Institution.

lacking in earlier attempts to produce long-playing records—a permanent stylus with a small tip radius to play the finely cut grooves.

A war of speeds began in 1949 when RCA introduced a seven-inch Vinylite record designed for 45 rpm to be played on a specially designed phonograph. After nearly two years of confusion, most manufacturers adopted the LP for classical music and albums; the 45 for short popular selections, especially for use in jukeboxes.

How did this revolution affect the world of music? With twenty-five–thirty minutes available on one LP disc, it became feasible to record entire operas and other long classical works. With the combination of high-fidelity equipment and the LP record, more people listened to classical music than ever before—without the distraction of frequent record changes. Music lovers replaced entire libraries of bulky 78 albums with the more compact new releases.

119

THE LISTENING CENTER

Most high-fidelity enthusiasts prefer systems made up of components. A typical system includes a turntable and a pick-up cartridge that converts the motions of the needle into minute electric impulses that are applied to the preamplifier and amplifier, enabling them to drive the speaker. Since the late 1950s, systems usually include two speakers to reproduce stereophonic recordings cut with two distinct channels of sound. Many include an FM tuner and a tape deck. After transistors began to replace vacuum tubes in the 1960s, the amplifier, preamplifier, and tuner were often combined into a receiver.

Although "golden ears" may agree on the superiority of the component system, they differ widely on the specific products that make up an ideal one.

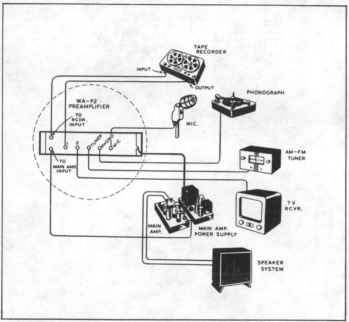

This 1956 drawing shows various components and how they should be connected to the preamplifier. From Heathkit Co.

A component system of the early 1950s. Gift of Dr. Walter J. Kaplan. Rek-O-Kit turntable, catalog number 330,464. Pickering cartridge. Sun Radio preamplifier and amplifier, 330,465. ElectroVoice speaker, 330,463.

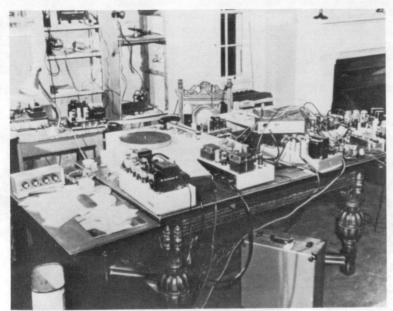

This 1953 listening room of a confirmed high-fidelity buff represents an extreme example of the change from console to component systems. From High Fidelity.

Other listeners hide the speakers in existing furnishings, such as this china cabinet. From High Fidelity.

Picture of a component system of 1970 showing how compact the electronic equipment and the speakers can be. From Acoustic Research, Inc.

The FM radio, developed by Major Edwin Armstrong, brought into living rooms broadcasts of high fidelity never before possible. Shown above is the Budapest String Quartet being broadcast live on FM from the Coolidge Auditorium at the Library of Congress in Washington, D.C., about 1961.

COMPONENT SYSTEM

Early component systems were put together by enthusiasts willing to try their soldering and carpentry skills. The "do-it-yourself" instinct among audiophiles of the 1950s was reminiscent of the early days of radio.

TAPE RECORDING

Magnetic-tape recording has probably influenced the lives of musicians more since World War II than did the phonograph fifty years earlier.

The amateur can readily record home performances, while the ease of editing tape allows the professional more flexibility in recording sessions and moviemaking. The best of several takes can be spliced together for the final master tape. Special effects are created by dubbing in several performances on one tape. These characteristics convinced broadcasters to record programs on tape by the 1950s.

Without the editing, dubbing, and fidelity made possible by tape machines, composers and performers would not have been able to create the entirely new style of electronic music of the past twenty years.

In a modern recording session, many microphones are used to transmit the sound to tape machines which are monitored by engineers at complex control panels. From RCA Records.

TELEGRAPHONE

Although Emile Berliner and the Volta Laboratory of Alexander Graham Bell experimented with magnetic recording, the first to develop a commercially successful machine was Valdemar Poulsen, a Danish engineer. On his Telegraphone, the variations in current set up by speaking into a transmitter are recorded on a steel wire or band as it is rotated between the poles of an electromagnet. Although Poulsen claimed that the quality of the reproduction was superior to that of the phonograph, the Telegraphone was not used by musicians for recording.

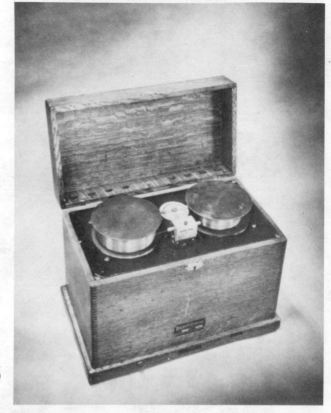

The Telegraphone. Made about 1907 by American Telegraphone Co., Springfield, Massachusetts. Catalog number 311,750. (Lautman photo 77187.)

Detail of the Air-King wire recorder. (Lautman photo 77361.)

WIRE RECORDER

Various attempts were made throughout the 20th century to market Poulsen's invention. By the 1940s some newsmen were using wire recorders for interviews. By the 1950s mail-order catalogs listed them for home use.

But wire did not lend itself to editing and was difficult to repair. The development of magnetic tape in Germany, and its acceptance and further development in this country after World War II, ended wire recording.

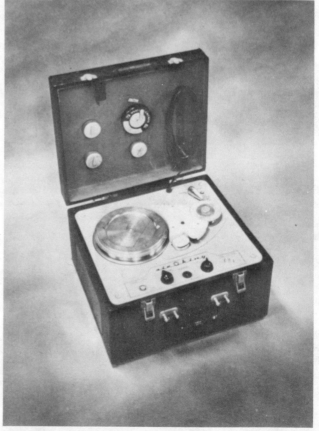

Air-King wire recorder, 1949. Made by Air-King, Brooklyn, New York. (Lautman photo 77360.)

MAGNECORDER

Representative of the earliest professional magnetic-tape
recorders manufactured in this country, the
Magnecorder was used mostly by professionals—who
still prefer a reel-to-reel machine that moves the tape
at a speed of 7½ inches per second (ips) or, even better,
15 ips. The Ampex reel-to-reel machine was also a
favorite of the professionals from its earliest days in
the 1950s.

The Magnecorder, 1952. (77135-C.)

Studio scene with Ampex in use.

*Cassette. Photo shows compact size for
ease of installation.*

CASSETTE-TAPE RECORDERS

Cassette and cartridge-tape recorders are found in
homes and automobiles throughout the world. The
packages eliminate handling and wear of the tape,
provide extended periods of uninterrupted music, and
are easy to install. The cassette is a reel-to-reel
system, as compared with the cartridge's endless-loop
design.

In 1970 prerecorded tapes accounted for thirty
percent of the sales of recorded music, and the music
industry has predicted that this percentage will grow.
The "Dolby system"—a development that reduces
tape hiss and noise even at the slow speed of
1¾ ips—has increased the fidelity of music on tapes
to make them serious competitors of discs.

MUSIC   "Save the Life of My Child"—Paul Simon
[Paul] Simon and [Arthur] Garfunkel, vocal, 1970.
Columbia KCS-9529.

"Aquarius" from *Hair*—Gerome Ragni and James Rado,
Galt MacDermot
Broadway cast, 1968.
RCA Victor LSO-1150.

"Have You Ever Been (to Electric Ladyland)"—Jimi
Hendrix.
Jimi Hendrix, vocal and guitar, 1970.
Reprise (Warner Bros.-Seven Arts Records, Inc.) 6307.

ELECTRONIC INSTRUMENTS AND MUSIC

The quest for new sounds led to amplified electric versions of familiar instruments and to totally new devices on which music could be composed as well as performed.

Electric guitar played by Alvin Lee of "Ten Years After" at the 1969 Woodstock Festival, the historic gathering of a half million young people in New York State. By permission of Warner Brothers and "Ten Years After."

REVOLUTION IN SOUND

A new music arrived when the composer and performer joined with the engineer to use electronically produced sounds. Reports of experiments by America's Thaddeus Cahill and his Telharmonium excited the European composer, Ferruccio Busoni, who wrote in 1907 that "music is born free; and to win freedom is its destiny. . . . In the new great music, machines will also be necessary."

Through the decades, many devices have been invented to produce music electronically. Some, like the Theremin and the electric organ, require a performer, who makes music from a limited source of sound prescribed by the inventor. Others, like the synthesizer, offer the composer virtually unlimited sound possibilities to realize on tape.

Performers, who at first feared they would be replaced by tape machines, find that many experimental composers include them, either to play traditional instruments (sometimes with electronic transformations) or electronic machines especially constructed for concert use.

Electronic and recording devices, at first designed for experimental composers, have also been used skillfully and imaginatively by popular-music groups. Though differing in content, popular and electronic studio music share techniques and machines that represent a revolution in sound.

Some of the electric equipment needed for the Telharmonium is shown: the power source, a group of inductor alternators (above), from McClure's Magazine, July 1906; tone-mixing transformer (below), from Electrical World, March 10, 1906.

Telharmonist at the keyboard. From *Electrical World, March 10, 1906.*

TELHARMONIUM

Some may have laughed when the telharmonist sat down at the keyboard of the Telharmonium in the early 20th century, but many musicians did not. Hearing the music electrically produced by Thaddeus Cahill's invention, they proclaimed it the beginning of a new era when composers would at last be freed from the limitations of existing instruments.

Known also as the Dynamophone, the invention—installed in Telharmonic Hall, New York—was ingenious, if unwieldy. Pressing the keys caused current produced by dynamos to be converted into musical sound. The nearly 200 tons of electric equipment, consisting of a power source, gears, shafts for more than 140 dynamos and tone mixers, was placed in the basement to isolate the noise of the machinery.

Cahill not only sought to generate but also to distribute music electrically. Transmitted by telephone, music from the central station could be heard by subscribers in restaurants, hotels, and homes. Some music distributors today, like Muzak, still use this principle of telephonic transmission as well as broadcasting.

From keyboards in the central station (above), Telharmony was heard in hotel lobbies similar to the one at right through a speaker hidden in the hanging basket of ferns and vines. From "Telharmony," a promotional brochure published by the New York Electric Music Co.

THEREMIN

By the 1920s Leon Theremin, a Russian-born scientist, had invented an apparatus with an electronic oscillator to produce musical tones. The performer could vary the pitch by moving his right hand toward or away from a perpendicular metal rod. The volume could be controlled by moving the left hand near a metal loop.

In 1929 RCA Victor manufactured the Theremin and a combination Theremin-phonograph. That same year, in New York, Joseph Schillinger—a Russian-born musician and mathematician—wrote the *First Airphonic Suite* for Theremin and orchestra.

Lucie Bigelow Rosen at the theremin in the music room of her New York home in the 1930s. From the Walter and Lucie Rosen Foundation, Inc.

Detail of a theremin, showing the oscillators. Made about 1929 by RCA Victor Co., New York. Gift of Mrs. Ralph Richards. (Lautman photo 77363.)

A concert for two theremins and accompanying musicians. Leon Theremin is performing at left. From Clark Collection, Smithsonian Institution.

HAMMOND ORGAN

The Hammond organ was developed in the late 1920s. This instrument had the advantage of producing and amplifying electronically more than one note at a time. As a substitute for the pipe organ in churches and homes, it was popular with amateurs and entertainers but had little influence on experimental electronic music.

Ethel Smith, one of the most popular electronic-organ players, at the Hammond organ. From Hammond Organ Co.

ELECTRIC GUITAR

Even in the 1920s the Gibson Company, manufacturers of the traditional guitar referred to today as the "acoustic guitar," began experimenting with amplified guitar sound. In the 1930s amplified guitars with a "singing tone" were advertised in mail-order catalogs. These were popular with groups playing Hawaiian and country music.

But as the pace of life quickened, the noise level rose. By the 1940s club entertainers playing blues and country music found that they needed to amplify their music to be heard above the customers' din. Today, players capitalize on the amplification and some have also developed new techniques of performance that produce sounds unique to the electric guitar.

Advertisement for "Singing Guitar" in Sears catalog of 1940. From Sears, Roebuck & Co.

Amplified western music has been enjoyed for years by patrons of rodeos, fairs, dances, and hotels in the West and Middle West. Shown here are Hadley Barrett and the Westerners in the 1950s at the Veterans of Foreign Wars Hall in Ogallala, Nebraska. From collection of Hadley Barrett.

A rock band in action with all its electronic equipment.

Muddy Waters transferred his Mississippi-Delta style of "bottleneck"-guitar playing to the electric guitar in the 1940s when he performed for Chicago audiences. He is shown here at the 1969 Smithsonian Festival of American Folklife.

A 1959 photo of the RCA electronic synthesizer at the Columbia-Princeton Electronic Music Center in New York. From RCA.

The Buchla Box.

RCA SYNTHESIZER, MOOG, AND BUCHLA BOX

While electronic music is a worldwide phenomenon, the idea of a single machine to create and combine electronic sounds more easily originated in America.

Developed about 1955, the RCA Electronic Music Synthesizer at the Columbia-Princeton Electronic Music Center in New York City is capable of generating electronically all of the physical characteristics of any audible sound, in any desired combinations. The system is operated by a coded-paper record, punched by the synthesizer at a keyboard resembling a teleprinter.

Smaller machines, like those developed in the 1960s by Robert Moog and Buchla Associates, are arranged in modules that have greater commercial possibilities. The Moog is equipped with a keyboard, which helps musicians bridge the gap between electronics and musical composition. Some have even become virtuoso performers on the instrument.

Composer Chris Swanson working with Moog equipment in the Moog studio, Trumansberg, New York, in 1970. From R. A. Moog, Inc.

ELECTRONIC MUSIC STUDIO

American composers began to experiment in earnest with electronic music in the 1950s. At first, the equipment was simple, often just tape recorders to record and transform the improvised sound of flute, piano, or voice.

In the early 1960s a well-equipped university electronic-music studio began to acquire several sine/square wave oscillators; voltage-controlled oscillators; a white-noise generator; microphones; a record player; several variable-speed tape recorders; filters; mixers, power amplifiers and speakers; and miscellaneous cables, wires, and furniture. The maze of wires and the complexity of creating music by splicing together short taped sections of sound discouraged many composers.

By the mid- to late 1960s most electronic studios were again more compact, thanks to newly developed equipment. By combining many of the functions of the sound generators and mixers into convenient modules, such companies as Robert Moog and Buchla Associates have made the composition of electronic music more accessible.

Conductor Leopold Stokowski. His interest in electronic music, starting with the Telharmonium in 1906, led him to schedule in 1952 the first American public performance of music for tape recorder by composers Vladimir Ussachevsky and Otto Luening.

Scores for electronic music.

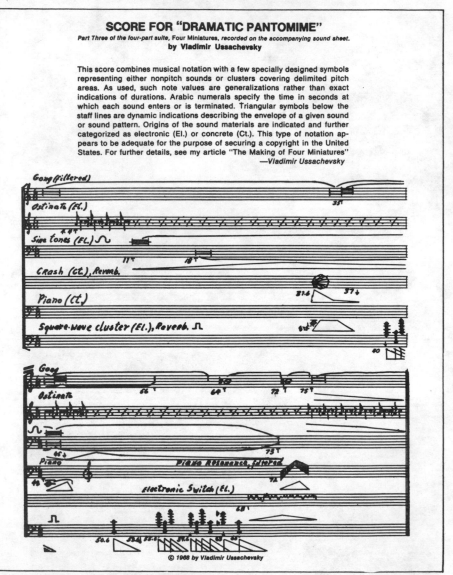

"Dramatic Pantomime" by Vladimir Ussachevsky, Columbia-Princeton Electronic Music Center. From Music Educators Journal, *November 1968. © Vladimir Ussachevsky.*

ITERUM FUGUE

Composer: William Serad, Eighth grade

My fugue, as in all fugues, has counterpoints (four to be exact) in a rather simple form, since a fugue is said not to be a form but rather a *texture.* The form (or texture) could best be expressed in the Latin saying, *A minima ad maximis ad minima* (from smallest to greatest to smallest). The title, *Iterum,* from the Latin, means "again." I chose this because of the repetition of the counterpoints. To break the boredom I broke section B down to three B sections. I included a few ultra-small episodes to keep the piece like a fugue, but in one respect there is a small difference from a fugue by Bach. My composition has no overlapping of subject and answer because it has no subject and answer at all.

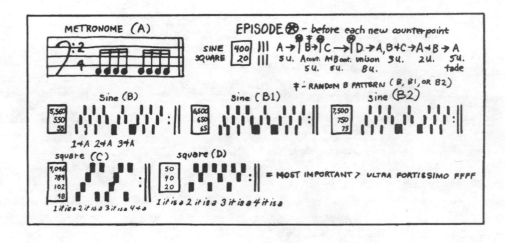

"Iterum Fugue" by William Serad, eighth-grade, Laboratory and Demonstration School, Philadelphia. From Music Educators Journal, November 1968.

An electronic music studio at Catholic University of America, Washington, D.C. From Emerson Myers.

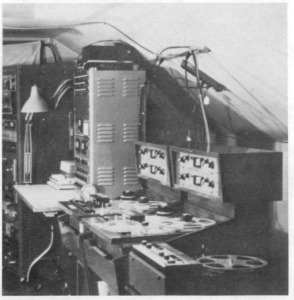

BIBLIOGRAPHY

Baker, Ray Stannard. "New Music for an Old World." *McClure's Magazine,* vol. XXVII, no. 3 (July 1906), pp 291-301.

Barnouw, Erik. *A History of Broadcasting in the United States.* 3 volumes. New York: Oxford University Press, 1966-1970.

Begun, S.J. *Magnetic Recording.* New York: Murray Hill Books, Inc., 1949.

Beishuizen, Piet. *The Industry of Human Happiness.* London: International Federation of the Phonographic Industry, 1959.

Blesh, Rudi, and Harriet Janis. *They All Played Ragtime.* New York: Oak Publications, 1966.

Bowers, Q. David. *Put Another Nickel In.* Vestal, New York: Vestal Press, 1966.

Charters, Samuel. *The Bluesmen.* New York: Oak Publications, 1967.

Clough, Francis F., and G. J. Cuming. *The World's Encyclopaedia of Recorded Music.* 3 volumes (covering 1925-1955). London: Sidgwick and Jackson Ltd., 1950-1955.

Gaisberg, Frederick William. *The Music Goes Round.* New York: MacMillan, 1942.

Gelatt, Roland. *The Fabulous Phonograph from Tin Foil to High Fidelity.* Philadelphia and New York: J. B. Lippincott, 1955.

Givens, Larry. *Re-Enacting the Artist.* Vestal, New York: Vestal Press, 1970.

Godrich, John and Robert M. W. Dixon. *Blues and Gospel Records, 1902-1942.* Revised edition. London: Storyville Publications, 1969.

High Fidelity, The Magazine for Audio-Philes, (summer 1951 to present).

Hughes, Langston, and Milton Meltzer. *Black Magic: A Pictorial History of the Negro in American Entertainment.* Englewood Cliffs, New Jersey: Prentice-Hall, Inc., 1967.

Jacobs, Lewis. *The Emergence of Film Art.* New York: Hopkinson and Blake, 1969.

——————. *The Rise of the American Film: A Critical History.* New York: Columbia University Teachers College Press, 1939, 1948, 1967.

JEMF Quarterly. John Edwards Memorial Foundation, Folklore and Mythology Center, UCLA, (October 1965 to present).

Knight, Arthur. *The Liveliest Art: A Panoramic History of the Movies.* New York: Mentor, 1957.

Koenigsberg, Allen. *Edison Cylinder Records, 1889-1912.* New York: Stellar Productions, 1969.

Kouwenhoven, John A. *Made in America.* New York: Doubleday, 1948. (Paperback edition: *The Arts in Modern American Civilization.* New York: Norton, 1967).

Malone, Bill C. *Country Music, U.S.A.* Austin: University of Texas Press, 1968.

Mattfeld, Julius. *Variety Music Cavalcade 1620-1950.* New York: Prentice-Hall, 1952.

Music Educators Journal, November 1968. (Special issue on electronic music.)

O'Connell, Charles. *The Other Side of the Record.* New York: Knopf, 1947.

Ord-Hume, Arthur, W. J. G. *Collecting Musical Boxes and How to Repair Them.* New York: Crown Publishers, 1967.

The Phonogram, A Monthly Magazine devoted to the Science of Sound and Recording of Speech, January 1891;-March, April 1893.

The Phonoscope, A Monthly Journal Devoted to Scientific and Amusement Inventions Appertaining to Sight and Sound, 1896-1899.

Read, Oliver, and Walter L. Welch. *From Tin Foil to Stereo: Evolution of the Phonograph.* Indianapolis: Howard W. Sams & Co., Inc., 1959.

Roehl, Harvey N. *Player Piano Treasury.* Vestal, New York: The Vestal Press, 1961.

Sandoz, Mari. *The Christmas of the Phonograph Records.* Lincoln: University of Nebraska Press, 1966.

Schuller, Gunther. *Early Jazz: Its Roots and Musical Development.* New York: Oxford University Press, 1968.

Settel, Irving. *A Pictorial History of Radio.* New York: Citadel Press, 1960.

Sheldon, Robert, and Burt Goldblatt. *The Country Music Story: A Picture History of Country and Western Music.* Indianapolis: Bobbs-Merrill, 1966.

Smart, James. *The Sousa Band: A Discography.* Washington, D.C.: Library of Congress, 1970.

Sousa, John Philip. "The Menace of Mechanical Music." *Appleton's,* September 1906.

Springer, John. *All Talking! All Singing! All Dancing!* New York: Citadel Press, 1966.

Walker, Leo. *The Wonderful Era of the Great Dance Bands.* Berkeley, California: Howell-North Books, 1964.